Lynn Sutin
15 Oct 2010

Self Realization
in Kashmir Shaivism

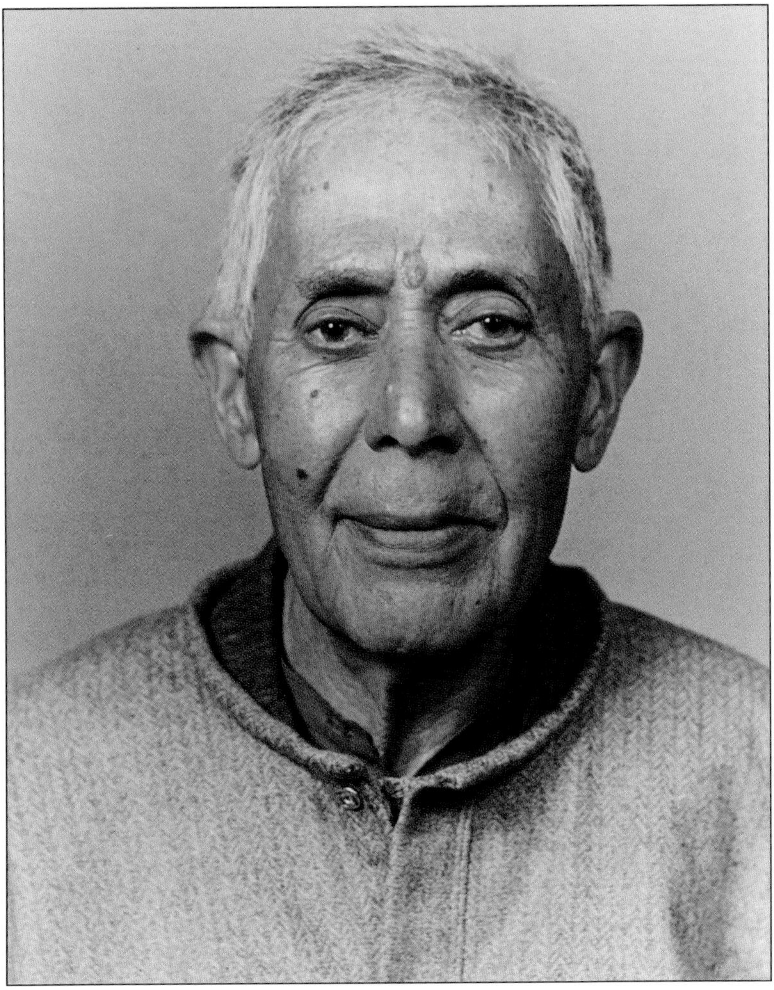

Self Realization in Kashmir Shaivism

The Oral Teachings of Swami Lakshmanjoo

JOHN HUGHES

Foreword by Lance Nelson

State University of New York Press

Published by
State University of New York Press, Albany

Printed in the United States of America

For information, address State University of New York Press,
State University Plaza, Albany, NY 12246

Production by Cathleen Collins
Marketing by Nancy Farrell

Library of Congress Cataloging-in-Publication Data

Lakshmanjoo, Swami, 1907–1991.
Self realization in Kashmir Shaivism : the oral teachings of Swami Lakshmanjoo / John Hughes : foreword by Lance Nelson.
p. cm.
Translated from Kashmiri.
Includes index.
ISBN 0–7914–2179–1
1. Spiritual life—Kashmir Śaivism. 2. Kashmir Śaivism—Doctrines. I. Hughes, John, 1942– .
BL1281.1552.L35 1994
294.5'4—dc20 94–29824
CIP

10 9 8 7 6 5 4 3 2

This book is dedicated to
my beloved Denise

The following English words exemplify the pronunciation of selected Sanskṛit vowels and consonants. The Romanized Sanskṛit vowel or consonant is first listed and then an English word is given to aid you in its proper pronunciation.

a	as	a in America.
ā	as	a in father.
i	as	i in fill, lily.
ī	as	i in police.
u	as	u in full.
ū	as	u in rude.
ṛi	as	ri in merrily.
ṛī	as	ri in marine.
e	as	e in prey.
ai	as	ai in aisle.
o	as	o in stone.
au	as	ou in house.
ś	as	s in sure.
ṣ	as	s in shun, bush.
s	as	s in saint, sin.

Contents

Illustrations

Foreword

> Thanks to him the oral tradition, after an apparent eclipse, has been securely renewed, because the Swami, a very learned scholar but also a real *yogin* and *jñānin*, has mystically lived that which the old Śaiva masters of Kashmir, and in particular Abhinavagupta, brought to light.
>
> —Lilian Silburn[1]

I still vividly recall coming across, as an undergraduate during the late sixties, a small book by Paul Reps entitled *Zen Flesh, Zen Bones*. This genuine spiritual classic continues to have wide appeal today. What most especially stuck in my mind then, in addition to Reps's sensitive retelling of 101 delightful Zen stories, was the account of his visit to the Kashmir Valley, known because of its mountainous beauty as the "Switzerland of India." There he discovered what he felt was an important pre-Zen text, the *Vijñāna Bhairava Tantra*, a central scripture of Kashmir

1. "Grâce à lui la tradition orale, aprés une apparente éclipse, s'est renouée solidement, car le swāmi, très savant *paṇḍit* mais aussi véritable *yogin* et *jñānin*, a mystiquement vécu ce qu'exposérent les anciens maîtres śivaïtes du Cashemire et, en particulier, Abhinavagupta" (Lilian Silburn, trans., *Hymnes de Abhinavagupta*, Publications de l'Institut de Civilisation Indienne, fasc. 31 [Paris: Èditions E. de Boccard, 1970], 1). (Translations from French and Sanskrit are my own.)

Śaivism. I remember being fascinated and, in a mysterious way, elevated by Reps's paraphrase of that short but profound work, which he called, from the practice it describes, "Centering." Somehow, however, I was even more captivated by Reps's description of his encounter with the saint who introduced him to the text and provided him with a translation, Swami Lakshmanjoo. As I reread Reps's words now, I experience again the emotional, intellectual, and spiritual pull that led me eventually to graduate studies in Indian philosophy. Reps begins:

> *Wandering in the ineffable beauty of Kashmir, above Srinagar I came upon the hermitage of Lakshmanjoo. It overlooks green rice fields, the gardens of Shalimar and Nishat Bagh, lakes fringed with lotus. Water streams down from a mountaintop.*
>
> *Here Lakshmanjoo—tall, full-bodied, shining—welcomes me. He shares with me this ancient teaching. . . . I see Lakshmanjoo gives his life to its practice.*[2]

This was my first encounter with this extraordinary Śaiva saint.

A Spiritual Magnet in the Vale of Kashmir

During my years in graduate school, I made a point of keeping close tabs on developments in the modern Hindu tradition. Again the presence of Lakshmanjoo crossed the horizon of my concern as I became aware that a number of Hindu spiritual leaders, including Swami Muktananda Paramahamsa and Maharishi Mahesh Yogi, were making a point of visiting and paying their respects to this Śaiva master during visits to Kashmir. My curiosity was aroused.

Although my research focus was on Advaita Vedānta, of which I had made a thorough study, I was becoming increasingly aware of nondual Kashmir Śaivism as expressing a more profound mystical realization. Put briefly, classical Advaita achieves its nond-

2. Paul Reps, *Zen Flesh, Zen Bones: A Collection of Zen and Pre-Zen Writings* (New York: Anchor Books, n.d.), 159–160.

Plate 1. Swami Ram, Swami Lakshmanjoo's Grand Master.

uality by denying the reality of objective existence, which is excluded from its statically conceived Absolute. It aims ultimately for a state of isolation (*kaivalya*) in pure spirit, from which the world is obliterated. Śaivism, on the other hand, offers a more thoroughgoing nondualism in which the universe is accepted—and experienced—as divine Consciousness itself in dynamic motion. This allows the Śaiva *yogin* to enjoy the Infinite as a vivid, vibrant reality at the level of the senses.[3]

As I continued my study of the literature on Kashmir Śaivism, I began to notice Lakshmanjoo's name appearing regularly in prefaces, dedications, and footnotes in the works of scholars writing in various languages. They were acknowledging, however briefly, their indebtedness to this Śaiva master. Among the who's who of Western scholars of Śaivism who spent time studying with Lakshmanjoo were the late Lilian Silburn and her colleague André Padoux, both of whom had distinguished careers as scholars of Tantrism at the Centre National de la Recherche Scientifique, Paris; Alexis Sanderson, currently Spaulding Professor of Eastern Religions and Ethics at Oxford University; and Mark S. G. Dyczkowski, an important younger scholar of Śaivism associated with Sampurnananda Sanskrit University, Benares. Other South Asianists who made the pilgrimage to Lakshmanjoo's Ishvara Ashram on the shores of Dal Lake include Professors Harvey P. Alper, J. G. Arapura, Bettina Bäumer, Gerald J. Larson, and K. Sivaraman. In addition, I became aware that in India itself Lakshmanjoo was held in high esteem by a distinguished circle of Hindu scholars in the holy city of Benares, several of whom traveled to his ashram seeking a more profound understanding of Śaiva doctrine and practice. This group of Tantric savants included Pandit Rameshwar Jha and Thakur Jaideva

---

3. See Paul Eduardo Muller-Ortega, *The Triadic Heart of Śiva: Kaula Tantrism of Abhinavagupta in the Non-dual Śaivism of Kashmir* (Albany, N.Y.: State University of New York Press, 1989), chaps. 1–2; also Lance E. Nelson, "Reverence for Nature or the Irrelevance of Nature? Advaita Vedānta and Ecological Concern," *Journal of Dharma* 16 (July–September 1991): 282–301.

Singh, the latter well-known for his valuable translations of Kashmir Śaiva texts. For many years, both scholars were in the habit of going to Kashmir during the summer to study with Lakshmanjoo.[4]

Silburn, who dedicated her life to the study of Hindu Tantrism, produced several important translations and studies of Kashmir Śaiva texts, including *Kuṇḍalinī: The Energy of the Depths.*[5] In preparing her translations, she studied with Lakshmanjoo during visits to Kashmir over a period of some twenty years. During that time she came to regard Lakshmanjoo as her "master in the science of Bhairava [Supreme Reality]."[6] Her description of her first visit to Kashmir conveys something of her feeling for the place and her relationship with Swamiji:

> *In 1948 I journeyed to India for the first time and met Swami Lakshmanjoo in Kashmir. I received from him some help in understanding the* Śivasūtra, *its commentaries, and also the* Spandakārikā *and the* Vijñānabhairava, *which I had attempted to translate.*
>
> *That year I lived near him in an abandoned hut of beaten earth on the uninhabited hills that dominate Dal Lake, toward which the terraces of the garden of Nishat descend [from the hills] by stages. I lived several months by myself at the heart of this exceptional site, in which the starkness of the rocky mountains, the subtle softness of the light, and the often hazy stillness of the lake joined together to create a harmony and a peace that was profound, yet pregnant—it seemed—with the*

---

4. Mark Dyczkowski, "An Appreciation of Jaideva Singh," in Jaideva Singh, trans., *The Yoga of Vibration and Divine Pulsation: A Translation of the Spanda Kārikās with Kṣemarāja's Commentary, the Spanda Nirṇaya* (Albany, N.Y.: State University of New York Press, 1992), ix, xiii.

5. State University of New York Press, 1988.

6. "Mon maître en Bhairavaśāsana" (Lilian Silburn, trans., *Le Vijñāna Bhairava*, Publications de l'Institut de Civilisation Indienne, fasc. 15 [Paris: Èditions E. de Boccard, 1961], 3).

Plate 2. Swami Ram with Swami Lakshmanjoo's mother and father.

> *presence of the great Śaiva masters who probably frequented that place.*[7]

Acknowledging that she had benefited greatly from Lakshmanjoo's vast knowledge of the Tantric tradition, Silburn expressed

7. "En 1948, je fis un premier voyage en Inde et rencontrai au Kaśmīr le swāmi Lakshmanjoo. Je recueillis auprès de lui des éclaircissements sur les Śiva sūtra, leurs gloses ainsi que sur la Spandakārikā et le Vijñānabhairava dont j'avais entrepris la traduction.

"Près de lui j'habitais cette année-là une hutte de terre battue abandonnée sur les hauteurs désertes qui dominent le lac Dal vers lequel s'abaissent par paliers les terrasses du jardin de Nishad. Je vécus plusieurs mois, solitaire, au coeur de ce site exceptionnel où la nudité de la montagne rocheuse, la douceur subtile de la lumière et l'immobilité souvent vaporeuse du lac s'allient et se fondent en une harmonie et une paix profondes encore imprégnées, semble-t-il, de la présence des grands maîtres śivaïtes qui fréquentèrent probablement cet endroit" (Lilian Silburn, trans., *Śivasūtra et Vimarśinī de Kṣemarāja*, Publications de l'Institut de Civilisation Indienne, fasc. 47 [Paris: Institut de Civilisation Indienne, 1980], foreword).

her profound gratitude to him for his untiring help with her work.[8]

As the result of his visits to Kashmir, Pandit Rameshwar Jha developed a profound devotion to Swamiji, to whose spiritual power he attributed certain spiritual realizations that he enjoyed. This is evidenced in his "Hymn to the Preceptor" (*guru-stuti*), a Sanskrit poem filled with lavish praise of Lakshmanjoo and his lineage of masters. For example: "I bow to the feet of the divine Lakṣmaṇa, nectar to [my] eyes, whose glorious power as the great Lord Śiva is incomprehensible to the intellect. Blessed by his compassionate glances, I shine here with the form of the universe."[9] Elsewhere in this hymn, Jha expresses his belief that Lakshmanjoo was a reincarnation of Lakṣmaṇagupta, a *guru* of Abhinavagupta.[10] Although not all of Lakshmanjoo's disciples share this opinion (some prefer to identify their master with Abhinavagupta himself), this hymn is still chanted daily by followers in Kashmir and elsewhere.

The extent of Jaideva Singh's indebtedness to Lakshmanjoo can be gauged by looking at the dedication pages of his translations. Attesting to his esteem, Singh wrote that Lakshmanjoo "unsealed my eyes." He spent hours with Swamiji—whom he regarded as "the doyen of Śaivāgama"—going over texts word by word before submitting them for publication. Singh's translation of the *Pratyabhijñāhṛdayam* is dedicated "with profound respect to Svāmī Lakṣmaṇa Joo, to whom I owe whatever little I know of Pratyabhijñā philosophy."[11] At the time he studied with Laksh-

---

8. Silburn, *Hymnes de Abhinavagupta*, 1; idem, *Le Vijñāna Bhairava*, 5.

9. *tasyāpratarkya-vibhavasya maheśvarasya pādau namāmi nayanāmṛta-lakṣmaṇasya / devasya yasya mahataḥ karuṇākaṭākṣair ālokito 'ham iha viśva-vapur vibhāmi* (vs. 18; Rameshwar Jha (Śrī Rāmeśvarācārya), *Śrīgurustuti* [Śrīnagar: Īśvara Āśrama, c. 1975], 6).

10. vs. 21; Jha, *Śrīgurustuti*, 7.

11. Jaideva Singh, trans., *The Yoga of Delight, Wonder, and Astonishment: A Translation of the Vijñāna-bhairava* (Albany, N.Y.: State University of New York Press, 1991), v, xxiii; idem, *Yoga of Vibration*, v; idem, *The Doctrine of Recognition: A Translation of the Pratyabhijñāhṛdayam with an Introduction and Notes by Jaideva Singh* (Albany, N.Y.: State University of New York Press, 1990), v.

manjoo, Singh was in his seventies, a respected scholar with already more than half a dozen books to his credit. Still, we are told, he gave reverent attention to the teachings of one whom he evidently regarded as his spiritual preceptor. "It was a moving sight," Dyczkowski reports, "to see this fine old man sit before his revered teacher with the simplicity of a young child."[12] A photo of Singh with Lakshmanjoo appears after the title page in the Indian edition of his translation of Abhinavagupta's *Parātrīśikā-vivaraṇa.*[13]

Perhaps the most vivid description of a scholar's encounter with Lakshmanjoo comes from Dyczkowski, who spent a good deal of time with Swamiji, beginning in the mid-1970s. His account reveals something of the attraction that Lakshmanjoo exerted over serious students of Tantrism: "Swamiji would rise early [in the] morning and we, his few Western disciples, would come to try and share, as best we could, in Swamiji's immense profundity. His exposition of the great works of the ancient Kashmiri masters—Abhinavagupta, Utpaladeva, and Kṣemarāja—would fill us with wonder."[14]

Scholar and Practicing Mystic

In such testimony we may well find the answer to the question of why practically all scholars who had a serious interest in nondual Śaivism were making the pilgrimage to the valley of Kashmir to spend time studying with Lakshmanjoo. There are three factors that begin to explain Swamiji's importance for students of Tantra.

First, he is to be distinguished from the typical yogī or swāmī in respect of his scholarly training and achievement. Nowadays it is common for Hindu monks to have only a minimal knowledge of

12. Dyczkowski, "Appreciation of Jaideva Singh," ix, xii.

13. Jaideva Singh, trans., *Parātrīśikā-Vivaraṇa: The Secret of Tantric Mysticism*, ed. by Bettina Bäumer; Sanskrit text corrected, notes on technical points and charts dictated by Swami Lakshmanjoo (Delhi: Motilal Banarsidass, 1988), v.

14. Dyczkowski, "Appreciation of Jaideva Singh," ix.

Plate 3. Swami Mehtabkak, Swami Lakshmanjoo's Master.

Sanskrit. This does not, of course, diminish their spiritual attainments, but it does mean that their acquaintance with the classical texts in the original language is limited. Necessarily, then, they have even less familiarity with the scholastic commentarial literature. While information about Lakshmanjoo's life and training is difficult to come by, it is clear that he was a genuine scholar of no mean attainment. Silburn must have had the opportunity to learn something of her preceptor's background during her long apprenticeship. She remarks: "Very young he decided to dedicate his life to the Trika; he studied texts and manuscripts under the tutelage of two of the best scholars of the time, Hara Bhaṭṭa Śāstrin and Rājānaka Maheśvara, acquiring in this way a deep and extensive knowledge of all the branches of Kashmir Śaiva philosophy and mysticism." Regarding Lakshmanjoo's language ability, she testifies: "Profound and sure is his knowledge of Sanskrit, and wide his learning concerning the various Śaiva systems of Kashmir. Many times in the past his translations and interpretations of particularly difficult passages were certified for me by that eminent Sanskritist, the late Louis Renou."[15] What makes such testimony remarkable is that Silburn was herself a distinguished Sanskritist and scholar. Although certainly not a devotee,[16] she had found in Lakshmanjoo a masterful guide to the scriptural tradition she wished to penetrate.

During his career, Lakshmanjoo demonstrated his scholarly interest and capacity by editing several important Sanskrit texts of the Kashmir Śaiva tradition, published in Srinagar and Benares. These include the *Bhagavadgītārthasaṁgraha* of Abhinavagupta (1933), the *Śrī Kramanayadīpikā* (1958), and the *Śiva-*

15. "Très jeune il décida de consacrer sa vie au Trika; il étudia textes et manuscrits auprès de deux des meilleurs *paṇḍit* du temps: Hara Bhaṭṭa Shāstrin et Rājānaka Maheśvara, acquérant ainsi une science profonde et étendue dans toutes les branches de la philosophie et de la mystique śivaïte cachemirienne" (Silburn, *Hymnes de Abhinavagupta*, 1); "Profonde et sûre est sa connaissance du sanscrit, et grande son érudition en ce qui concerne les divers systèmes śivaïtes du Cachemire. A maintes reprises dans le passé ses traductions et interprétations de passages particulièrement difficiles m'ont été confirmées par le sanscritiste éminent qu'était Louis Renou" (Lilian Silburn, trans., *Hymnes aux Kālī la Roue des Énergies Divines*, Publications de l'Institut de Civilisation Indienne, fasc. 40 [Paris: Institut de Civilisation Indienne, 1975], foreword).

16. She evidently went against Lakshmanjoo's advice in publishing certain material on *kuṇḍalinī*, complaining that he regarded it as "a rather daring undertaking" (Lilian Silburn, *Kuṇḍalinī: The Energy of the Depths* [Albany, N.Y.: State University of New York Press, 1988], xvi). Probably, as an authentic tantric, he thought some of the information unsuitable for public distribution.

sotrāvalī of Utpaladeva (1964).[17] Swamiji could speak Sanskrit fluently, and delighted in the opportunity when he found someone with whom he could converse in the sacred language. Like other traditionally trained *paṇḍits*, he had a prodigious memory and could quote verse after verse by heart from a wide range of sources in support of points he was making in conversations or lectures. He also had a scholar's mind for detail, if we can judge from certain of Singh's remarks. For example, when Singh was working on his translation of the *Spandakārikā*, Swamiji not only provided him with a "luminous exposition" of the text, but helped him on a more practical level by correcting misprints in the printed edition. Lakshmanjoo, while helping Singh with his translation of the *Pratyabhijñāhṛdayam*, saved him immense labors by tracing the sources of the numerous quotations in the text. Any reader of Singh's translation of the *Vijñāna-bhairava* will come across notes in which the translator records alternate meanings, and alternate readings of the text, supplied by his mentor.[18] Lakshmanjoo contributed to Singh's translation of the *Parātrīśikāvivaraṇa* by providing numerous textual emendations, based on manuscripts available in the valley and oral tradition. He also dictated notes and charts elucidating technical matters discussed in the work and composed a Sanskrit dedication. In her collection of translations of Abhinavagupta's hymns, Silburn indicates that she decided not to include a certain text, even though it was in the standard edition. This was because Lakshmanjoo—exercising a critical awareness uncommon in traditional scholars—judged it to be not from the great master's own hand.[19]

---

17. *Bhagavadgītārthasaṁgraha: Śrīmad Bhagavad Gītā with Commentary by Mahāmaheśvara Rājānaka Abhinavagupta*, edited with notes by Pt. Lakshman Raina Brahmacārī (Srinagar, 1933); *Śrī Kramanayapradīpikā* [portions of the *Kramastotra*, of uncertain authorship], edited with Hindi translation by Rājānaka Lakṣmaṇa (Srinagar, 1958); *The Śivastotrāvalī of Utpaladevāchārya with the Sanskrit Commentary of Kṣemarāja*, edited with Hindi commentary by Rājānaka Lakṣmaṇa, Chowkhamba Sanskrit Series, No. 15 (Varanasi: Chowkhamba Sanskrit Series Office, 1964).

18. Singh, *Yoga of Vibration*, xxiii; idem, *Doctrine of Recognition*, 1; idem, *Yoga of Delight*, xxiii, 50, 62, 63, 111, 128.

19. Silburn, *Hymnes de Abhinavagupta*, 2.

All this being so, it remains that the "immense profundity" that attracted Dyczkowski and other scholars is not to be explained by Swamiji's scholarship alone. There was a second factor: students of Tantra came to the ashram at Nishat Bagh because they saw in Lakshmanjoo much more than a mere *paṇḍit*. By all accounts, he was a practicing *yogin* of considerable attainment. Scholars from academic settings removed geographically from the home of the living tradition found in Lakshmanjoo, it seems, what they could not find in printed texts or the *paṇḍits* of Benares. Silburn's estimate of Lakshmanjoo as a *yogin* and *jñānin* (realized sage) as well as a scholar, given above, is echoed by Baümer. She describes him as "the only living representative of the full Kashmir Śaiva tradition both in its theory and practice, *śāstra* and *yoga*."[20] The implication, of course, is that Swamiji had himself undergone the transformative discipline recommended by the texts. Dyczkowski writes of Lakshmanjoo: "He was an immense inspiration to me as a living example of Kashmiri Śaivism in practice." That he was a yogic adept was apparent, to sensitive onlookers, even in his exposition of the texts. "Somehow he sees much more in them," Dyczkowski reports, "than could ever be grasped through mere bookish knowledge and we could all feel that behind his words lay another dimension beyond them in which he lived and from which he beckoned us to join him."[21]

Last Master of the Oral Tradition

The final reason for Lakshmanjoo's importance to scholars was one that may have sometimes, in its historical urgency, overshadowed the others. Lakshmanjoo was, by most accounts, the last and only living representative of the lineage of Kashmir Śaiva preceptors. He was thus the only remaining authentic cus-

20. Bettina Baümer, preface to Singh, *Parātrīśikā-Vivaraṇa* (Delhi, 1988), xi.

21. Mark S. G. Dyczkowski, trans., *The Stanzas on Vibration: The Spandakārikā with Four Commentaries* (Albany, N.Y.: State University of New York Press, 1992), ix; idem, "An Appreciation of Jaideva Singh," ix.

Plate 4. Swami Lakshmanjoo in his twenties.

todian of its oral teachings.[22] This understandably gave a certain edge to the scholars' quest. For example, Silburn writes: "It is my inestimable good fortune to have been able to draw from the knowledge of this great master, the last to possess the key to a doctrine among others most profound and mysterious."[23] It is perhaps in this light also that we should understand Swamiji's willingness to commit at least a portion of his knowledge to academicians: that it might be preserved for posterity.

Be that as it may, there can be no doubt that the scholars who came to Lakshmanjoo felt the need for a guide with access to the oral tradition. The Tantric traditions of India, like other esoteric traditions, are anchored in lineages involving direct communication of wisdom and experience from master to disciple. The transmission of knowledge, in the form of teachings and practical instructions, was originally and most authentically oral in nature. Although the practice of writing down some of this material had become accepted by the eighth century or earlier, the process was and continues to be regarded with some suspicion. The teachings and practices deal with yogic experiences that are extremely difficult to describe and differentiate for those who have experienced them, let alone those who have not. Even the more philosophical material written for a general scholarly audience—like the Pratyabhijñā literature—is filled with technical

---

22. Padoux describes Lakshmanjoo as "certainly the last depository of the teaching of the Trika, as it was transmitted from master to disciple for centuries" (sans doute le dernier dépositaire de l'enseignement du Trika tel qu'il a été transmis de maître à disciple depuis des siècles; André Padoux, trans., *La Parātrīśikālaghuvṛtti de Abhinavagupta*, Publications de l'Institut de Civilisation Indienne, fasc. 38 [Paris: Institut Civilisation Indienne, 1975]: 18). See also Archana Dongre, "Last Bhairava Master Will Teach until Year 2006," *Hinduism Today* (July 1991): 1; Paul Eduardo Muller-Ortega, foreword to Jaideva Singh, trans., *A Trident of Wisdom: Translation of Parātrīśikā Vivaraṇa* (Albany, N.Y.: State University of New York Press, 1989), x; idem, foreword to Singh, *Doctrine of Recognition*, ix; Singh, *Doctrine of Recognition*, 1.

23. "C'est la chance inestimable que nous avons eue de puiser ainsi dans la science de ce grand maître, le dernier à posséder la clef d'une doctrine profonde et mystérieuse entre toutes" (Silburn, *Le Vijñāna Bhairava*, 5).

terms that no one but trained specialists can understand. The Tantric texts are even less accessible. In addition to evoking the subtle nuances of yogic states, they prescribe for initiates religious attitudes and rituals that, in their radical world affirmation, sometimes run counter to conventional Hindu piety and mores. Moreover, the practices—particularly those associated with the rise of *kuṇḍalinī*—involve psychological and spiritual dangers that make expert guidance essential.[24] Thus on several levels Tantric literature carries the potential to be easily misunderstood, misappropriated, or both, by those inadequately prepared to receive it. The Tantric writers, therefore, feared potential abuse should this material fall into the hands of the uninitiated.

The result was that most of what these masters did write was obscure, whether because of the nature of the subject matter or through deliberate omission and obfuscation. Abhinavagupta, for example, sometimes intentionally cuts discussions short, declaring that the topic is secret and that he has already revealed more than he should. Scholars complain that his symbolic language can be interpreted on several levels simultaneously. Frequently, it is impossible to tell which meaning or meanings are appropriate.[25] The texts are, moreover, famous for their use of a highly technical jargon intelligible only to insiders, those who have been initiated into the practices and have acquired some experiential awareness of the spiritual realities described. Often, the meaning of key terms was kept secret; sometimes elaborate systems of coded language or "intentional" (*sandhā*) speech were employed. These texts were, in fact, written by and for a small, elite circle of preceptors and their dedicated disciples. Access to manuscripts, hand-copied and privately circulated, was limited. In addition to preparatory disciplines, initiation, and knowledge of the technical jargon, the texts presume above all the active, personal guidance of an authentic preceptor. The latter should be an individual formed by, and capable of transmitting, the esoteric wisdom of the tradition, handed down orally through his or her lineage.

24. See Silburn, *Kuṇḍalinī*, xiii.
25. Muller-Ortega, *Triadic Heart of Śiva*, 14–15, 62.

Given all this, we are not surprised to learn that Jaideva Singh was convinced that no one, not even the best Sanskritist, could properly translate Kashmir Śaiva texts without the assistance of a teacher versed in the tradition.[26] Noting the perplexing lacunae and obscurities that make these works so difficult to approach, Padoux concluded, "it is necessary in such matters to be guided."[27] The Indian tradition has attained an extraordinary level of literary achievement, to be sure. Still, it has never intended that the texts that elaborate its various branches of knowledge (*śāstras*) should function independently of an oral teaching tradition. The ideal of the scholar "self-educated" from books is foreign to the traditional Indian scene, as it is to other wisdom traditions. ("It is a grievous mistake," the Prophet Muhammad is reported to have said, "to take the written page as your *shaykh*."[28]) The notion of mastering a field of knowledge without relying on a preceptorial tradition is unthinkable in a culture still oral in its most genuine expression. As a result, almost all religious texts in India were written with the idea that they should be read in the context of the spoken commentary of an authoritative teacher. In such a setting, the written manuscript functions more as an outline or point of departure than final authority. The latter rested with the *guru*.

Such attitudes are, of course, even more pronounced in the Tantric tradition, which seeks to protect a wisdom that is profound but vulnerable to misuse. As Brooks points out: "Axiomatic to the study of esoteric Tantric texts is the necessity of oral interpretation by living initiates; too much in texts is obscured by difficult language or is designed to exclude the uninitiated . . . in every case, the presence of the living *guru* is assumed to be the final arbiter of tradition."[29] Because of their deliberately obscure

---

26. Dyczkowski, "Appreciation of Jaideva Singh," xiii.

27. Padoux, *La Parātrīśikālaghuvṛtti*, 16.

28. Labib al-Sa'id, *The Recited Koran: A History of the First Recorded Version*, trans. and adapted by Bernard Weiss, M. A. Rauf, and Morroe Berger (Princeton, N.J.: The Darwin Press, n.d.), 54; quoted in William A. Graham, *Beyond the Written Word: Oral Aspects of Scripture in the History of Religion* (New York: Cambridge University Press, 1987), 104.

29. Douglas Renfrew Brooks, *Auspicious Wisdom: The Texts and Traditions of Śrīvidyā Śākta Tantrism in South India* (Albany, N.Y.: State University of New York Press, 1992), xvi.

nature, Tantric texts more than any others become intelligible only within the horizon of an oral culture that renders them accessible. Scholars who approach these texts, no matter how good their preparation linguistically and otherwise, inevitably become aware very early on of their need to avail themselves of what Brooks calls "the 'missing' oral component that accompanies texts" in the Tantric milieu.[30]

All this supports John Hughes, the editor of the present volume, in his decision to describe the contents of chapters one and three ("Fifteen Verses of Wisdom" and "Entrance into the Supreme Reality") as "renderings." Although they represent Swami Lakshmanjoo's expositions of two traditional Kashmir Śaiva texts, they are more than mere translations. They capture at least the verbal portion of a multi-level encounter among text, master, oral tradition, student, and environment. The reader must imagine the text itself being spoken, often chanted, vibrating the minds and hearts of the students as the sacramentally potent voice of the *guru*. The students, thus empowered, are profoundly engaged. It is important, of course, that they themselves are practicing the teachings and are open to some experience of the realities being uncovered. As Anne Klein reminds us in her recent study of oral teaching in the Tibetan tradition, the aesthetic and emotional tone of the setting itself also makes a significant contribution to the discourse.[31] In our case, the environment is Kashmir, ancient home of Vedic seers and Śaiva masters. Outside is the lotus-filled jewel of Dal Lake; the snow-capped peaks of the Himalayas form the horizon; the air is vibrant and crystal clear. In the hermitage of Lakshmanjoo the students sit in the worship hall around their preceptor, with images of their master's master, and his master's master—the links of the lineage—silently showering blessings from the walls behind.

In this complex network, the central and most important node is, of course, Lakshmanjoo, the *guru*. An extraordinary human being, he himself is multidimensional, embodying the obvious value of years of scholarship, as we have seen, but also the more

30. Brooks, *Auspicious Wisdom*, 9.

31. Anne Carolyn Klein, *Path to the Middle: Oral Mādhyamika Philosophy in Tibet* (Albany, N.Y.: State University of New York Press, 1994), 5–6.

intangible attributes associated with yogic realization. Above all he makes present and accessible in living form the precious secrets of the oral Śaiva tradition he has inherited. The master's "renderings"—two of which are made available in this volume—have thus a range that significantly exceeds the compass of the text itself, for they are products of the living interaction of text, master, oral tradition, student, and environment. The mere text comes expansively alive as it is catalyzed by its participation in this many-faceted process.

In Swamiji's lectures—as presented here in chapters 2, 4, and 5—the focus on a particular text is, of course, absent. The rest of this potent teaching network, however, remains in place as the master guides the students through the whole range of the Kashmir Śaiva tradition. He weaves his scholarship and his spiritual experience together with the oral tradition of his predecessors. We become, if we so chose, the privileged auditors.

Lakshmanjoo's Śaiva Lineage

Swami Lakshmanjoo traces his lineage back to the great Kashmir Śaiva polymath Abhinavagupta (tenth–eleventh centuries C.E.) and beyond.[32] Śaivism had flourished in the Kashmir Valley for several centuries before the time of Abhinavagupta, and it continued to thrive for several hundred years after. The nondual Śaiva teaching was passed down through illustrious preceptors such as Somānanda (tenth century C.E.), his pupil Utpaladeva, and Utpaladeva's pupil Lakṣmaṇagupta, who—as mentioned above—was one of Abhinavagupta's preceptors. Also worthy of mention are Kṣemarāja (eleventh century), a disciple of Abhinavagupta, and Jayaratha (twelfth century), who commented on the great master's masterpiece, the *Tantrāloka*.

There is little reliable information on the recent history of Śaivism in Kashmir. However, it seems that the advent of Islam in the valley in the fourteenth century, combined with weaknesses within Hindu society itself, caused the tradition to go into

32. Swami Lakshmanjoo, *Kashmir Shaivism: The Secret Supreme* (Albany, N.Y.: State University of New York Press, 1988), 89–95.

Plate 5. Swami Lakshmanjoo at fifty.

decline. Periods of tolerance under enlightened Muslim rulers alternated with periods of persecution. All but the Brahmans eventually converted to Islam, temples were destroyed, and a good number of Sanskrit texts were lost forever. By 1907, when Lakshmanjoo was born, the Kashmir Valley had for centuries been predominantly Muslim. Although the Hindus that were left remained strongly Śaiva in orientation, there were increasingly fewer authentic teachers, and probably still fewer worthy aspirants, left to carry on the tradition.

Still, in the late nineteenth century there were two important Śaiva masters in the valley. Swami Manakak, regarded by Kashmiris as an exalted saint, was—like many preceptors of the Śaiva lineage—a householder. His disciple, Swami Ramjoo (d. ca. 1914) is said to have been born a *siddha* (realized Tantric adept). Like his master, Swami Ram was held in utmost esteem by his contemporaries.[33] It is reported that he was in the habit of remaining in yogic trance (*samādhi*) for four hours at a time.[34] Among his devotees was Narain Dass, a devout Śaiva householder and successful businessman. Narain Dass established Swami Ram in a large house at Fatehkadal, Srinagar, which became the latter's ashram. As John Hughes explains in his introduction to the present volume, Swami Lakshmanjoo was Narain Dass's son. Before Swami Ram's death, the master entrusted the seven-year-old Lakshman to the tutelage of his senior disciple, Swami Mehtabkak. Such were the beginnings of this extraordinary spiritual career.

After a long and immeasurably valuable life, Swami Lakshmanjoo left his body on September 22, 1991, at the age of eighty-four, leaving numerous disciples and admirers to mourn his passing. Thanks to the dedicated labors of John Hughes and his wife Denise, hours upon hours of Swamiji's teaching have been preserved on audio and video tape for posterity. This collection promises to be of tremendous value to students of Tantra—scholars and practitioners alike. The tapes are slowly being transcribed by devotees and edited for publication. This book is an early outcome of this process, following *Kashmir Śaivism: The Secret Supreme* (SUNY Press, 1988), and it is hoped that many more volumes of Swamiji's teachings will follow.

The question of who will carry the tradition after Lakshmanjoo must, of course, be asked. Its urgency is heightened by the conflict in contemporary Kashmir between India and various Muslim separatist groups, among the tragic effects of which has been the dislocation of the Hindu community. In May 1991 Swamiji gave Viresh Hughes, the then thirteen-year old son of John and Denise, the traditional *upanayana* ceremony, his rite of initiation as a Hindu. Shortly thereafter, a few months before his passing, Lakshmanjoo named Viresh his successor. Young Viresh was born in Kashmir, but has lived in the United States since

33. Samsar Chand Kaul, "The Institutions of Kashmir Saivism," in *Aspects of Kashmir Śaivism* by B. N. Pandit (Srinagar, Kashmir: Utpal Publications, n.d.), 233.

34. Jha, Śrīgurustuti, 2.

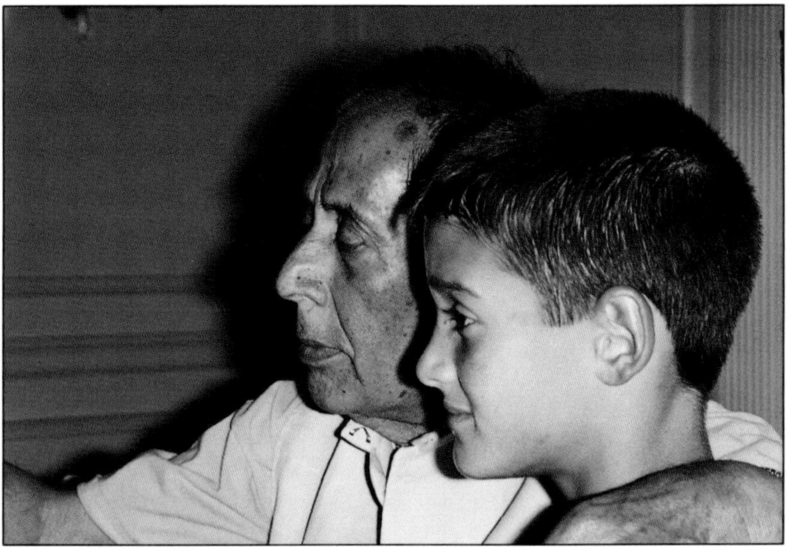

Plate 6. Viresh Hughes with Swami Lakshmanjoo in 1991.

1986. Now that Swamiji has left his body, it is not immediately clear how this young American will receive the proper training. In response to the natural concern of devotees, Swamji did say cryptically, "It will happen automatically."[35] What exactly he meant is not clear to his followers. There are a good number, however, who believe that their master remains active, from a spiritual plane, even after his physical departure.

Conclusion

Practitioners will certainly be awaiting further indications of how Lakshmanjoo's influence will continue to express itself. Meanwhile, there can be no doubt of the importance of the Kashmir Śaiva vision to the ongoing stream of human spirituality. We can only be thankful to John Hughes and the State University of New York Press for making available the full, authentic voice of this tradition's most genuine modern exponent. Lakshmanjoo is a

35. Dongre, 25.

presence too valuable to remain hidden in notes and acknowledgments appended to scholarly translations.

I should say that, while I cannot claim myself to have studied with Swami Lakshmanjoo, I did have the opportunity to meet him on several occasions, both in Kashmir during the late 1970s and in the United States just before his passing. I remember well a particular discussion I had with him. My question concerned the differences between Śaiva nondualism and Śaṅkara's Advaita Vedānta. In response, Lakshmanjoo described the Śaiva *yogin's* power to elevate his or her perception of objective reality so the universe "shines" as the dynamic movement of the Supreme Consciousness itself. What struck me most profoundly was his metaphor for this extraordinary power of transmutation. He called it "digesting the world." I somehow felt that here was a teacher who knew in the most profound sense what he was talking about.

Lance E. Nelson
University of San Diego

Acknowledgments

Above all I want to express my unending gratitude and devotion to my master, Swami Lakshmanjoo, who believed in me and charged me with the task of making his teaching live. Swamiji was a man of exceptional kindness and understanding who, during the many years that I studied under him, never tired of explaining and clarifying the difficult, and many times hidden, teachings of Kashmir Shaivism. It is due to his boundless patience and compassion that this book is possible.

I want to thank the many well-wishers who, being interested in having Swamiji's lectures and translations preserved and published, have given me unending encouragement and support to begin this challenging and demanding task.

During the preparation of this book Lance Nelson continually provided me with insight and support. Though very busy with his work, he was always ready to read and reread this book's manuscript as it passed through different stages of completion. His suggestions, recommendations, and counsel have proved to be immensely valuable.

George van den Barselaar, while visiting from Australia, provided many suggestions and helped in the preparation of the introduction. George, a very close devotee of Swamiji, spent many years in Kashmir. While he was there he served Swamiji intimately and became quite familiar with his history and the stories surrounding his life. His willingness to share his memories and insights helped immensely in the preparation of the introduction.

I am indebted to Jagdish Sharma for the important contribution he provided by correcting the Sanskrit contained in this volume. For many years Dr. Sharma was the resident Sanskrit Scholar for the Universal Shaiva Trust which was located in Kashmir just near Swamiji's Ashram. During that time he worked directly under Swamiji's guidance. Even though the trust is no longer active, Dr. Sharma continues his work supervising the transcribing of Swamiji's English lectures and translations from audio tape media and correcting the Sanskrit in these transcriptions. This is really a demanding task, and I am deeply grateful for the valuable work he is doing.

In helping me to determine the timings of important events and for providing me with hitherto unavailable photos of Swamji I am very grateful to Shibanji Kaul. I also want to express my appreciation to Mohan Kishen Watal, who—being filled with devotion and singleness of purpose—worked long and hard to translate Swamiji's lectures on "Practice and Discipline" from the original Kashmiri into English.

For their unending support and financial help, without which my many years in Kashmir would not have been possible, I want to thank my mother and father. I want to thank my wife Denise, my daughter Shanna, and my son Viresh for their breakless encouragement and support. We are living this adventure together.

Introduction

The Context

Kashmir Śaivism is a magnificent system of spirituality which, since its inception, has emphasized not only the understanding of its concepts but the direct realization of its truth. According to its devotees, truth cannot be grasped by mere intellect; it can only be apprehended through direct experience. Because Kashmir Śaivism regards itself as a practical system of spiritual realization, it has come to place great emphasis on its oral tradition, preserving and passing on the understanding that is indispensable as a guide to the direct, living apprehension of its truth.

Most recently, the oral tradition of Kashmir Śaivism has been preserved and strengthened in the person of Swami Lakshmanjoo Raina. Swamiji (as he is known to his devotees and students) had a profound understanding of this great spiritual way; he was an extraordinary man whose whole life was dedicated to his beloved Śaivism. Swamiji fully imbibed the teachings and practices of Kashmir Śaivism and was looked upon as the embodiment of kindness, compassion, and generosity. He was a selfless devotee of God. His life was marked by a continual remembrance and outpouring of love for Lord Śiva, whom he worshiped in the form of Amriteśvara Bhairava, the lord of the nectar of liberation.

Swamiji was born as Lakshman Raina in Srinagar, Kashmir, on May 9, 1907. He was the fifth child in a household of four boys and five girls. Swamiji's birth came about through unusual circumstances. By the time Swamiji's eldest brother Manju Das had reached the age of eighteen, his mother had given birth to three more daughters but no sons. His parents wanted to have another boy. They approached Swami Ram, their family *guru*, and asked him to give them something special, something magical, so they could have another son. Wanting very much to help, Swami Ram blessed an almond and gave it to Swamiji's mother to eat. Having great faith in Swami Ram's spiritual powers, she ate the almond and soon afterwards became pregnant. When she gave birth to a son everybody was overjoyed. Hearing about this birth, Swami Ram became very excited and immediately asked to be taken to their house. It was common knowledge that Swami Ram had lost the use of his legs, but upon taking the baby in his arms he entered into an ecstatic mood and began dancing about singing, "I am Rama and he is Lakshmana."[1]

Swami Lakshmanjoo was a great being who truly lived an exemplary life in perfect accordance with the spiritual path of Kashmir Śaivism. But he was also human. By understanding his human side the teachings in this book will resonate more powerfully for the reader whether he or she comes out of intellectual curiosity or with the desire to realize Kashmir Śaivism in their own lives.

Meeting the Master

My wife and I first journeyed to Kashmir in the spring of 1969, along with Maharishi Mahesh Yogi and a group of his Western students. During our stay Swami Lakshmanjoo gave a discourse to our group on Kashmir Śaivism. As a graduate student of Indian philosophy and religious studies, I was intrigued by this impressive speaker and the relatively unknown philosophy he spoke about.

In 1971 I returned to Kashmir along with my wife Denise and

1. This is in reference to the story of the divine incarnation of Rāma and his brother Lakṣmaṇa as told in the classical Indian text the *Rāmāyaṇa*.

Plate 7. Swami Lakshmanjoo with Ramana Maharshi.

daughter Shanna to learn from Swamiji the philosophy and practical teachings of Kashmir Śaivism. Although I still knew very little about Kashmir Śaivism I knew it was a tradition that emphasized realizing and experiencing the supreme truth in the context of one's own life. Furthermore, I knew deep down that if I wanted to learn the secrets of Kashmir Śaivism I needed to study with a teacher who not only understood the tradition, but had practically experienced its fruit and truth in his own life and being. My research convinced me that Swami Lakshmanjoo was such a man. He was, at the time, the last living master of the Kashmir Śaivaite tradition; that is, he was the last in a line of masters/disciples whose spiritual genealogy was marked by direct oral transmission of the secrets of Śaivism. Being the last living *guru* of Kashmir Śaivism meant that Swamiji held the pure distillation of a rich spiritual tradition.

I traveled with my wife and daughter to India, harboring the

Plate 8. Swami Lakshmanjoo with Maharishi Mahesh Yogi.

profound hope that Swamiji would share the philosophy and secrets of Kashmir Śaivism with me. Of course, I did not know what to expect from such a great philosopher and saint. Although I hoped that he would respond to my heartfelt request, I was totally unprepared for, and even overwhelmed by, the deep kindness, consideration, and enthusiasm with which he honored our visit and my request.

After we had arrived in Srinagar and settled into our hotel, I told Denise that I was anxious to meet with Swami Lakshmanjoo as soon as possible. I had written him six months earlier about my intention to travel to Kashmir to learn Kashmir Śaivism. In the letter I said that I hoped he would agree to teach me. Here I was in Kashmir, and I still had not received a reply from him. For all I knew he would refuse my request. Perhaps he would not even meet with me. My mind was filled with unpleasant possibilities. I was really nervous and had no idea what to expect. It was Sunday afternoon when I took a taxi around the edge of Dal Lake to Swamiji's *ashram* (hermitage).

Sunday was a public day. When I arrived the *ashram* was filled with people of all ages and genders. The devotees of Swami Lakshmanjoo were sitting and standing in groups talking among themselves. Swami Lakshmanjoo, whom everyone referred to simply as Swamiji, was nowhere in sight. When I asked his whereabouts I was told that he had just gone up to his room and would be returning shortly. As I waited for his return my excitement and nervous apprehension increased. Some of the devotees waiting in the garden were quite friendly and expressed a keen interest in my situation. They began to shower me with questions—who I was, how old I was, what I wanted, how long I was going to stay, how I had heard of Swamiji, and so on. Being involved in this intense session of questions and answers, I hardly noticed that quite a bit of time had passed. Then off to my right in the direction of Swamiji's house I noticed a commotion. One of the devotees standing with me said that Swamiji had come down.

I saw him stepping down from the porch of his house. He was taller than I remembered, surrounded by devotees and moving in the direction of his lecture hall. He seemed to be really enjoying the day. He was thin and about six feet tall. He was neatly dressed in the traditional Kashmiri dress, which I learned was called a *pharon*. He certainly had a look about him that expressed power and inner strength. I don't know how else to say this, but to me he seemed kingly in stature and bearing. His appearance was further defined by his close-cropped hair and a face that was handsome and kind, beaming with friendliness and warmth.

One of the devotees went up to him and told him that I had arrived and would like a chance to meet him. He looked at me, turned to this devotee, and spoke to him briefly. This devotee then came up to me and told me that Swamiji had agreed to meet with me and that I should follow Swamiji to the lecture hall. I was so excited and nervous I could hardly stand it. Meeting someone of his stature and reputation was awe-inspiring.

When I entered the lecture hall he was already sitting down on the rug-covered floor. He looked up at me and told me to come near him and sit down. I moved near him and sat down where he pointed. Without a word he reached over, took my hand, looked me in the eyes, and said, "I am so very glad that you have come." Something instantly changed within me. I felt a great surge of love and gratitude. I knew that he was very different from anyone I had ever met. Without thinking I found myself saying, "Sir, I know that you are the Lord my God. Thank you for allowing me to come." He then reached into his pharon and took out the photograph of my family I had sent him over six months before. He showed me the photograph and said, "I've been waiting for you." This was my first—and by no means last—exposure to his great humanity. As time passed Swamiji's great spirit enveloped and uplifted my soul.

Swamiji not only agreed to teach Denise and me Kashmir Śaivism, but he also helped us find a place to live. He said that he was eager to share the wealth of Śaivism with us because he wanted to save it from being lost to future generations. He believed that the wealth of Kashmir Śaivism should be given to all people, regardless of caste, creed, gender, or color. He generously agreed to allow us to tape-record his discourses with the thought that they would be preserved and might subsequently be transcribed, edited, and eventually published.

I did not know it at the time, but we were to spend more than fifteen years in Kashmir, absorbing the wisdom and holiness of

Plate 9. Swami Lakshmanjoo with Swami Muktananda.

this extraordinary man. Eventually we would build a house next to Swamiji's; our daughter would be reared in Kashmir and attend the local Presentation Convent Girls' School; and in 1977 Denise would give birth to a son, whom Swamiji named Viresh.

Plate 10. Shankarpal Rock (The Rock of the Shiva Sutras*).*

The Setting

The home of Kashmir Śaivism is the valley of Kashmir, India, a region of breathtaking beauty. One hundred miles long and 75 miles wide at its broadest, and 5,500 feet above sea level, the valley is surrounded by majestic mountains. This terrain isolates Kashmir from the tropical Indian subcontinent, providing it with a mild and temperate climate. Since ancient times the Kashmir Valley has offered royalty and the wealthy a refuge from the oppressive heat of Indian springs and summers. It has been a haven to philosophers and the spiritually minded as well.

Swamiji's home was nestled against the mountain range at the southeast corner of the valley. Although his home was referred to as the *ashram* and had that pure and uplifting atmosphere common to holy places, it was actually his private residence. His home echoed the physical splendor of Kashmir. From his garden one could behold the panorama of the valley, the enchanting Dal Lake, and the edge of deep wilderness. In harmony with this natural beauty was Swamiji's careful touch upon the terrain. The grounds were carefully landscaped: green lawns were trimmed, flowers bloomed year-round, and fruit trees (especially apple) abounded. The house was well maintained, and was permeated by a simple, comfortable warmth. One looked forward to the seasonal changes, especially during the early morning hours when the air surrounding the *ashram* was filled with a wonderful variety of sweet fragrances.

A small distance from the main house was a hall where Swamiji met with his students and revealed through his discourses the sacred texts of Śaivism. The hall conveyed grace and reverence. Kashmiri carpets and colorful sheeting were stretched over the floor. Instead of chairs, throw pillows were scattered about for those who found sitting on the floor too difficult. One wall was filled with windows that invited the colors of the garden inside; the other walls were adorned with pictures of Swamiji, his master and grand master, his parents, Lord Śiva, and various saints of Kashmir and India. The room, like the man and the teachings, was timeless. Had this room existed a thousand years ago it would appear the same. The hall seemed to vibrate with the ageless wisdom and teachings of the Śaiva masters. It was in this hall that I received the teachings found in this book.

Once or twice a week for approximately two hours we would meet in the lecture hall. There was always a feeling of excitement and anticipation on these special mornings. A small group of between five and ten students would gather in the hall at 9:00 A.M. and sit in a small semicircle on the floor. Swamiji would then arrive and sit behind a small, low table, upon which he kept the particular text he was revealing. In this direct and proximate way, Swamiji taught us. What was most remarkable about these lectures, more even than the teachings, was the power of the teacher himself.

Swamiji's manner of teaching was traditional but inspiring. Although he lectured in English, the verses he explained were in Sanskrit, the traditional philosophical language of India. These verses possessed poetic meter and Swamiji would chant them before illuminating them in his discourse. His understanding of Sanskrit was profound. He could explain the most abstruse concepts with simplicity and elegance. As a boy he had learned Sanskrit in the traditional fashion by first memorizing and reciting the grammar (*Aṣṭādhyāyī*) composed by the great Sanskrit gram-

Plate 11. Swami Lakshmanjoo at seventy-five.

marian Pāṇini. Then he began to study the language from a Kashmir Śaivite point of view, coming to understand that the Sanskrit alphabet and language were actual expressions of reality. With a deep understanding of the fundamentals of the language, with the constant guidance of his master Swami Mehtabkak, and through his own experience, he was able to glean the special meanings hidden within the verses. In his discourses he made the philosophy and ancient myths vibrate with life and meaning. He did not speak as if he were talking about something separate and remote from himself; rather, his words described the very fiber of life and reality. They revealed a philosophy—and the greatness of the preceptor who imparted it.

Swamiji was extremely well read. He had, of course, a profound knowledge of the scriptures and philosophy of Śaivism, particularly Kashmir Śaivism. In addition, he had a wide-ranging knowledge of the traditional religious and philosophical texts of India. When translating he would freely draw on other texts and commentaries to further clarify, expand, and substantiate his teaching . He could recall the text by simply remembering the first few words of a verse. His mind was so clear and focused that he held countless verses in his active memory, and he could draw on them as needed. I once asked him if he ever forgot a verse. He replied, "If I see or read anything, I remember it."

His Life

In Kashmir each Hindu family has a priest who performs all their religious ceremonies and gives them advice on spiritual and religious matters. Swami Ram was Swamiji's family's priest. He was also Swamiji's grand master, that is, his *guru*'s *guru*.

Swami Ram was a householder. One fateful day a tremendous earthquake shook the valley of Kashmir, killing his wife and children. After many years had passed, he decided to remarry. His mother-in-law opposed his remarrying with great vigor, and Swami Ram considered her remonstrances as a direct sign from Lord Śiva. From that day he decided to give all of his effort to realizing God. He was single-minded in this effort and began to meditate for longer and longer periods. He would sit for days, motionless and deep in meditation. Finally, as a result of maintaining the meditation posture for such an extended period of time, he lost the use of his legs. Having reached the pinnacle of spiritual fulfillment, however, he remained unconcerned by this physical damage.

Swami Ram had great regard for Swamiji's father, Narian Dass,[2] and his mother, Arnimal, and they in turn had the greatest respect for him. They not only served him wholeheartedly, but Swamiji's father provided him with a house as well.

Swami Ram told Swamiji's parents that their son was destined to be a great spiritual soul. Throughout his remaining years Swami Ram kept a close eye on the young Lakshman. At the end of his life, when he was preparing to leave this world, he directed his closest disciple Swami Mehtabkak to watch over young Lakshman—to initiate him, teach him, and fill him with the world of Kashmir Śaivite spirituality.

Swamiji was seven years old when Swami Ram left this world. Even at this young age Lakshman would spontaneously enter into states of deep meditation. After Swami Ram passed away, the young Lakshman became a disciple of Swami Mehtabkak. Swamiji became single-minded in his devotion and service to his

2. Narian Dass, though a successful merchant and entrepreneur, was a very pious man. He owned mercantile stores that catered to the British, who traveled to Kashmir each spring and summer to escape the intense heat of the Indian plains. He was a progressive man who was always eager to find new ways to expand his enterprise. At that time the Maharaja had decreed that only people of Kashmiri origin could own land in Kashmir, a law that remains in force even today. This posed a particular problem for the British. Narian Dass became involved when British friends informed him about houseboats, a system that had long been used in the Netherlands. He immediately realized that Kashmir had sufficient lakes and rivers to support such a system. He also knew that houseboats would resolve the land ownership problem. So after some research and thoughtful planning, Narian Dass built his first houseboat. This was the beginning of the houseboat industry in Kashmir. His venture proved to be such a success that he soon entered the houseboat trade in earnest. To this day the now renowned houseboats give tourists a charming and colorful place to stay during their visits to Kashmir.

Plate 12. Swami Lakshmanjoo with some Kashmiri devotees.

master, asking nothing from him except the opportunity to serve him wholeheartedly. In time he became Swami Mehtabkak's closest disciple.

In India and Kashmir parents traditionally arrange the marriage of their children. When Swamiji was thirteen years old, his parents began to talk to him about getting married. Even though he was only thirteen, they wanted to begin the search for a suitable bride. In those days children were betrothed and married at a very young age. Swamiji told them that he had no desire to ever get married. He told them that his only desire was to dedicate his life to the realization of God. This made them worry. After all, if he didn't get married who would take care of him in his old age? They continued to pressure him. Prospective brides were brought in for his inspection and approval, but Swamiji continued to refuse. Finally his parents became desperate and tried to force him to marry.

To escape this pressure he decided to leave home. To ease his parents' dismay, he left a note telling them not to worry, that he was leaving in search of God. When they discovered the note his parents were frantic. They searched everywhere for him but to no avail. After some time a traveler passing through Srinagar reported that a young ascetic had been seen in a secluded forest known as Sadhu Ganga. The description of this young ascetic matched Swamiji's. His father, anxious to find his son, immediately set out for Sadhu Ganga. Upon reaching the forest his father was overjoyed to find his son there. He begged Swamiji to return home. Swamiji initially refused, but after much persuasion agreed to return. He, however, set down some conditions. First, his parents had to give up the idea of getting him married; second, he had to be given a place of his own to live. He told them that they must understand that his sole purpose in life was to serve his master and realize God.

Shortly afterward, his father purchased a beautiful plot of land on the mountainside near Nishat Bagh, a sixteenth-century Mughal garden overlooking Dal Lake. There he built a house where Swamiji could devote himself fully to his Lord without material hindrance.

In 1933, at the age of twenty-one, Swamiji published, along with Abhinavaupta's commentary, the Kashmiri recension of the *Bhagavad Gītā*. He continuously taught that since the presence of the Lord, who is the innermost center of each and every object, is everywhere, then everyone must therefore be essentially equal. He was totally opposed to the notion that one person was more qualified for spiritual growth than another. Caste, creed, gender, color, or religious belief was not a prerequisite for enlightenment. In his introduction to the *Bhagavad Gītā* Swamiji states: "Those commentators who would exclude the lower caste (*śūdras*) from liberation merely on the ground of their birth are foolishly mistaken in their interpretation of the Lord's message, which is universal and eternal." Throughout his life, beginning as a young man, he was tolerant, broad-minded, and universal in his thinking.

In time Swamiji's reputation spread. Spiritual leaders and scholars journeyed from all over the world to receive his *darśan* (blessing) and to ask him questions about various aspects of Kashmir Śaivite philosophy. He gained renown as a devotee of Lord Śiva and as a master of the nondual tradition of Kashmir Śaivism.

When Swamiji's father passed away he left his son with a respectable inheritance that allowed him to become financially self-sufficient. Throughout his life he never accepted money from anyone, nor did he ever charge fees or ask any compensation for his teaching. People often tried to give him gifts of money but he always refused. The only time he accepted monetary gifts was on the occasion of his master's death anniversary. The money he received was only used for his master's celebration, never for himself.

Swamiji taught that yogic powers were naturally gained on the path to God Consciousness. Both his master and his grand master had developed these powers but only used them to help people in need. He warned his devotees that such powers are a hindrance on the path to true spiritual realization; they can cause the aspirant to become sidetracked and to lose sight of the real goal. People usually came to Swamiji with philosophical questions or to have their spiritual experiences clarified. There were, however, those who came simply for help. Often they were from the poorer classes of Hindu or Muslim society, and they came to see Swamiji for many and varied reasons: a sick cow, an illness in the family, possession by evil spirits, a letter of recommendation for a job, even with the desire to conceive children. Swamiji never refused any sincere request. On many occasions he used his yogic powers, yet in such a way that the recipient was unaware of how his or her problem was resolved. Their faith in him was firm and they affectionately called him "Lal Sahib," or friend of God.

Every year, according to the lunar calendar, Swamiji would celebrate his birthday. It was always a festive occasion in late spring. People came from all over Kashmir and other parts of India to celebrate his birthday, and everyone was welcome. On this special day he had meals served to between 10,000 and 15,000 people. He provided everything and asked for nothing in return.

In India Hindu Brahmins traditionally are pure vegetarians. For reasons unknown, however, Kashmiri Brahmins eat meat. Throughout his life, however, even from the time he was a boy, Swamiji was opposed to eating meat. Once his mother tried to trick him into eating meat by telling him that meat came from trees. Even then he rejected it. She was so worried about him. She believed, as many did, that young boys needed to eat meat to remain healthy. She tried in many ways to get him to eat meat,

Plate 13. Swami Lakshmanjoo giving tikas *during one of his birthday celebrations.*

but he always refused. Swamiji would never eat at anyone's house unless they refrained from eating or cooking meat in the house for at least two weeks prior to his coming. This was a very strict rule from which he would not deviate.

Killing of any kind was abhorrent to this compassionate and saintly man. Many years ago I donated some money to purchase a sheep that was to be slaughtered and eaten at a celebratory dinner for a group of workers we employed. Swamiji found out about the purchase and subsequent slaughter of this sheep. He was deeply saddened by this event. Early in the morning he called me to his house. When I arrived he was agitated. He asked me, "Do you know what you have done in slaughtering this sheep? Last night when this sheep was slaughtered I felt his pain and anguish. He suffered so that I remained awake throughout the night experiencing this sheep's pain. How could you cause this kind of pain and suffering to an innocent animal who had done nothing to you? You did all of this violent action only to satisfy the sense of taste. What a sin this is." He then sent me away. Here was a man of unprejudiced sympathy and compassion not only for fellow humans but for all living things; a man of great faith, who generously tried to reveal the truth to others; a man of great personal strength, who understood the nature and scope of spiritual power.

Throughout his life Swamiji taught his disciples and devotees the ways of devotion and awareness. He shunned fame and recognition and did not seek his own glory. Swamiji knew Kashmir Śaivism was a most precious jewel and that by God's grace, those who desired to learn would be attracted to it. His earnest wish was that it be preserved and made available to all who desired to know it.

On September 22, 1991, at the age of eighty-four, Swamiji attained the great liberation (*mahāsamādhi*) and left his physical body. His friends and disciples felt a deep sadness because of the personal loss they experienced, but inwardly they rejoiced, for they knew that their beloved master was finally freed from the fetters of this world.

Textual Contents

Overview

This volume is divided into five chapters: The first, third, and fifth—*Talks on Practice, Talks on Discipline* and *The Secret Knowledge of Kuṇḍalinī*—contain original works by Swami Lakshmanjoo; the second and the fourth—*Fifteen Verses of Wisdom* and *Entrance into the Supreme Reality* are his renderings in English with traditional oral commentary of two small but important Sanskrit texts on Kashmir Śaivism, the *Bodhapañcadaśikā* and the *Parāprāveśikā*.

Talks on Practice and Talks on Discipline

The chapters entitled *Talks on Practice* and *Talks on Discipline* were taken from a series of lectures that Swamiji gave in 1980 near his home at the Śaiva Institute Hall in the village of Gupta Ganga.

During the fall of that year Swamiji suddenly wanted to give lectures on the practical aspects of meditation and discipline in

Kashmir Śaivism. He said that his purpose in giving these lectures was to reveal and establish the hidden yet practical teachings of this tradition.

In these talks he tells us that the nondual tradition of Kashmir Śaivism is something to be lived and experienced, not just thought about. It is not merely an intellectual exercise but a tradition where the truth of its teaching must be experienced to be known. He also demonstrates the connection between spiritual aspiration and moral discipline. In the *Talks on Discipline*, Swamiji talks about personal, ethical, and moral discipline and its importance for the spiritual seeker. We see how these various ethical and moral disciplines play both a descriptive and a prescriptive role in the life of the seeker. As descriptive they are evidence of the aspirant's readiness and qualifications; as prescriptive they form the basis for determining correct thought and action.

Swamiji gave these lectures in Kashmiri, the local language, over a period of three weeks in late October and early November. They were then transcribed and translated into English and finally edited for publication under Swamiji's guidance.

The Secret Knowledge of Kuṇḍalinī

Swamiji gave the lectures entitled *The Secret Knowledge of Kuṇḍalinī (Kuṇḍalinī Vijñāna Rahasyam)* at the Tantric Sammela (convocation), a gathering held in Varanasi (Benares) at the Sanskrit University on March 11, 1965. At the time he was not well known to either the Tantric or intellectual community of India. His lecture was not expected to be any different than the usual scholarly analysis of some aspect of Tantric lore. Instead, the audience was treated to something quite different. In his discourse he spoke about the heart of Tantric spirituality, the experience of *kuṇḍalinī*. The impact this lecture had on the audience was considerable, for in it he revealed heretofore little known mysteries of *kuṇḍalinī*. The *paṇḍits* of Benares were enthralled by the depth of his understanding of the Tantra and his experience of *kuṇḍalinī*. In this lecture he also revealed and clarified the Tantric understanding of the relationship of the Sanskrit language to reality. The organizing committee of the Tantric Sammela was so impressed with his grasp and comprehension of Sanskrit grammar and Tantric philosophy that they invited him to sit at the front of the convocation with the other official members of the gathering.

Fifteen Verses of Wisdom and Entrance into the Supreme Reality

The two Sanskrit texts, the *Bodhapañcadaśikā* and the *Parāprāveśikā*, which are rendered by Swamiji in the two chapters *Fifteen Verses of Wisdom* and *Entrance into the Supreme Reality*, are works by two very important Śaiva luminaries, Abhinavagupta and his chief disciple, Kṣemarāja.

The great Śaiva saint-philosopher Abhinavagupta lived in Kashmir toward the end of the tenth and the beginning of the eleventh centuries A.D. Throughout his life he sat at the feet of many learned teachers and masters and became proficient in all aspects of Indian philosophy and spirituality. He was an eminent scholar and teacher of Śaivism and possessed supreme knowledge of all matters relating to Kashmir Śaivism. His most famous work is the voluminous compendium of Tantric knowledge—including its practical and ritualist aspects, as well as the spiritual and philosophical—entitled *Tantrāloka* or *Light on the Tantra*. This work of thirty-six chapters is a textbook intended for masters.

The *Bodhapañcadaśikā* or *Fifteen Verses of Wisdom* is a brief but revealing collection of verses by Abinavagupta. As he tells us in the conclusion, this text was written to instantaneously elevate those dear and devoted disciples whose intellectual power was not highly developed. Swamiji was interested in explaining this text in English because it addresses the fundamental reality of nondual Śaivism and sheds light on the relationship of Lord Śiva to His creation. According to Abhinavagupta this universe, which is filled with infinite diversity, is not different or separate from the supreme light of Consciousness called Lord Śiva. The external objective world is nothing but the expansion of His Energy. It is filled with the glorious radiance of His God Consciousness. Thus, this world is not an illusion; it is completely real. In his rendering, Swami Lakshmanjoo unfolds the nature of this creation and the knowledge that frees us from our own self-delusion. His exposition lends clarity and understanding to this important work of Abinavagupta. The ideas he illumines are subtle and fundamental to understanding the central themes of Kashmir Śaivism.

The *Parāprāveśikā* or *Entrance into the Supreme Reality* is an illuminating and abstruse work by Abhinavagupta's chief disciple, Kṣemarāja. In this work Kṣemarāja introduces us to the various levels and aspects of this creation, from the subtlest to the grossest, from Lord Śiva to the element of earth. He shows us that, in reality, there is no difference between that which is subtlest and that which is grossest. In the world as seen by nondual Śaivism there is only the kingdom of Lord Śiva. After revealing the mechanics that comprise the full expansion of this creation, Kṣemarāja discloses that it is the supreme, sacred *mantra sauḥ* that "digests" this creation. It is through this *mantra* that disciples or aspirants are shown how to bring to an end the field of elements and, ultimately, rest in the element of Śiva.

In Conclusion

In this volume Swamiji takes us on a journey—a journey of discovery and rediscovery. Herein he reveals to us the reality of this world and our place in it. We learn that this world is not different from God. It is a world created by the Lord in play, for the fun of it. In creating this world God loses Himself in the world just for the joy and excitment of finding Himself. In actuality we are that Lord. Our great journey, therefore, is a journey of rediscovery filled with joy and excitement. The journey may seem long and the way uncertain, but great preceptors like Swamiji have gone before us. In these chapters Swamiji reveals the way, the means, and the end to light the path. To help us on our way, he draws us a mystical, spiritual map filled with his personal insight and experience.

ONE

Fifteen Verses of Wisdom

TODAY I AM GOING TO TALK ABOUT A SHORT text entitled "Fifteen Verses of Wisdom" (*bodhapañcadaśikā*) by Abhinavagupta, the great master of all aspects of Kashmir Śaivism. These fifteen verses provide a brief exposition, and capture the essence, of the doctrine of Kashmir Śaivism.

1. *The brilliance of the One Being's light does not vanish in external light or in darkness because all light and darkness resides in the supreme light of God Consciousness.*

The light of a candle is outshined by the light of the sun but the radiance of that One Being's light is not outshined by external light or overshadowed by darkness. This is because all external light and darkness reside in that Supreme light of Consciousness.

2. *This Being is called Lord Śiva. He is the nature and existence of all beings. The external objective world is the expansion of His Energy and it is filled with the glamour of the glory of God Consciousness.*

This One Being of infinite light is called Lord Śiva and the external collection which makes up the objective world is His

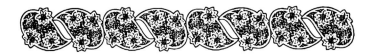

Energy (*śakti*). The external world is nothing more than the expansion of His Energy. It is not separate from His Energy. This Energy is filled with the radiance of the glory of God Consciousness. And so we see that Lord Śiva is the Energy holder, and the universal state of the objective field is His Energy, His Śakti.

> 3. *Śiva and Śakti are not aware that they are separate. They are interconnected just as fire is one with heat.*

If for the sake of explanation we make a distinction between Śakti and Śiva then one could say that Śakti is this whole universe and that from which this universe issues forth is Śiva. This Śiva and Śakti, Lord Śiva and this world, are not aware that they are separate. Why is this? Simply because in reality they are not separate at all. The state of Lord Śiva and the state of universe are one and the same, just as the fire is one with heat. Heat is not separate from fire; fire is not separate from heat.

> 4. *He is the God Bhairava. He creates, protects, destroys, conceals, and reveals His nature through the cycle of this world. This whole universe is created by God in His own nature, just as one finds the reflection of the world in a mirror.*

This universe is created by Lord Śiva in His own nature. The Lord protects and gives strength to the universe. The universe and the universe holder, i.e., the creator of universe, are one and the same.

This universe is a reflection (*pratibimba*) of Lord Śiva. It is not created in the same way as a woman creates a child, which at birth becomes separate from herself. Rather, this universe is created in the same way as the image of an object, such as a city, can be found reflected in a mirror. In the case of Lord Śiva, there is no city which exists independently of the mirror. The only thing that exists is the city seen in the mirror. There is no separate object reflected in the mirror, rather Lord Śiva creates this whole universe in the mirror of His own nature by His independence (*svātantrya*), His freedom.

5. *The collective state of the universe is His supreme Energy (*śakti*), which He created in order to recognize His own nature. This Śakti, who is the embodiment of the collective state of the universe, loves possessing the state of God Consciousness. She is in the state of ignorance, remaining perfectly complete and full in each and every object.*

Why has He created this supreme Energy in His own nature? He has done this for one reason—to recognize His own nature. This whole universe is nothing more than the means by which we can come to recognize Lord Śiva.

You can recognize Lord Śiva through the universe, not by abandoning it, but by observing and experiencing God Consciousness in the very activity of the world. If you remain cut off from the universe and try to realize God Consciousness, it will take centuries. But if you remain in universal activity and are attentive to realizing God Consciousness, you will attain it very easily.

So, in the universe there is ignorance and there is a way to get rid of this ignorance. This is the way of meditating in the activity of the world.

Lord Śiva creates this external universe for the sake of realizing His own nature. That is why this external universe is called Śakti, because it is the means to realize one's own nature.

When He was solely Śiva, He was in His full splendor of God Consciousness. He did not recognize His own nature because it was already there. But He wants His own nature to be recognized. And yet, because it is already there, there is nothing to recognize. Therefore, in order to recognize His nature He must first become ignorant of His nature. Only then can He recognize it.

Why should He want to recognize His nature in the first place? It is because of His freedom, His *svātantrya* (independence). This is the play of the universe. This universe was created solely for the fun and joy of this realization.[1] It happens that when His full-

1. This differentiation, which is the universe, has come out because of the overflowing of the ecstasy of God Consciousness. The ecstasy of God Consciousness overflows and the external universe flows out from His own nature.

ness overflows, He wants to remain incomplete. He wants to appear as being incomplete, just so He can achieve completion. This is the play of His *svātantrya*—to depart from His own nature in order to enjoy it again. It is this *svātantrya* that has created this whole universe. This is the play of Śiva's *svātantrya*.

This process is also known as *unmeṣa* and *nimeṣa*. *Unmeṣa* is the flourishing of that God Consciousness and *nimeṣa* is the withdrawal of that God Consciousness. *Unmeṣa* is expansion and *nimeṣa* is contraction. Śiva contains both of these states within Himself simultaneously.

At the time when His nature overflowed, Śakti[2] was in His own nature. Then He had to separate Śakti from His nature. In that state of separated Śakti, Śiva also exists. However, in that state Śiva is ignorant and wants, as He did before, to have the fullness of His knowledge.

The evidence that, while being in the state of ignorance, Śiva was already filled with knowledge is found in the fact that, at the moment He realizes His own nature and is filled with knowledge, He has the experience that the state of knowledge was already there.[3] So there was never really any separation. Separation only *seemed* to exist.

6. *The supreme Lord Śiva, who is all-pervasive and fond of playing and falling, together with the Energy of His own nature simultaneously brings about the varieties of creation and destruction.*

---

2. In the state of God Consciousness Śakti is complete, and in the state of ignorance Śakti is also complete. And yet, Śakti relishes possessing the state of God Consciousness. In each and every object She is complete, and in each and every object this completion is neither too little nor too much. In this external world, this completion is the same as it was in the state of the fullness of God Consciousness and the same as it was before the creation of the universe.

3. While experiencing an object, which is also in ignorance, in the field of ignorance, this experience is also full. But Śiva does not know this fullness and He does not know that He is full. He only knows this fullness at the time of realizing His own nature. And, when he realizes His own nature, this memory comes to His mind, "I was already full, so why was I meditating?"

This supreme Lord Śiva, who is all-pervasive, along with the Energy of His own nature, creates varieties of creation and destruction.

He creates birds, He creates bugs, He creates everything in this world. He creates whatever is possible and whatever is not possible. And He does not create it in succession. He creates it simultaneously (*yugapat*). But what is the purpose of all this? The purpose is to discover that God Consciousness also exists in all creation.

What is the Energy of His own nature? Universal existence, the universal cycle of universe. With this universal cycle Lord Śiva is fond of playing and also falling.

Take the example of a young boy. It may happen that when this young boy becomes too excited he begins to jump about wildly and may bump his head. In the same way God has masked his own nature because there is too much ecstasy. He wants to disconnect that ecstacy, but that ecstasy, in reality, cannot be disconnected at all. The Lord knows that, but still for His own amusement He temporarily disconnects it. Then, at the time when he again realizes His own nature, He feels that the ecstacy was *already* there.

7. *This supreme action cannot be accomplished by any other power in this universe except Lord Śiva, who is completely independent, perfectly glorious and intelligent.*

This kind of action can not be accomplished by any power in this universe other than Lord Śiva. Only Lord Śiva can do this. Only Lord Śiva, by His own *svātantrya*, can totally ignore and mask His own nature.

Lord Śiva wants, in His creation, to disconnect His God Consciousness completely and then to discover that it was never disconnected. Although it is disconnected, it is not disconnected. In the real sense it is not disconnected. This is the supreme action.

If you are full of life, how can you be without life? You cannot but Lord Śiva can. Lord Śiva can become without life. He can become completely insentient (*jaḍa*) and totally disconnected from God Consciousness, just like a rock. For where is the existence of Lord Śiva in a rock? In rocks there is nothing, it is just a rock.

This is His *svātantrya*, His glory, His intelligence. Intelligence does not mean that in this super-drama called creation you will only play the part of a lady or a man. With this kind of intelligence you will also play the part of rocks, of trees, of all things. This kind of intelligence is found only in the state of Lord Śiva and nowhere else.

8. *The limited state of consciousness is insentient and cannot simultaneously expand itself to become the various forms of the universe. The possessor of independence is absolutely different from that insentient state of consciousness. You cannot, therefore, recognize Him in only one way. The moment you recognize Him in one way you will also recognize Him in the other way.*[4]

In this super-drama of creation the limited state of consciousness can play the part only in an individual way. When it has taken the part of a rock it cannot simultaneously, at that moment, become a tree, a bird, a tiger, a human being, or the gods Brahma, Rudra, Viṣṇu, Īśvara, and Sadāśiva. However, Lord Śiva can. Simultaneously he has become all these forms and every form in the universe as well. This is the way He spreads and expands His own nature.

You know that an ordinary limited being who lives in one place cannot at the same time live in another place. This is not the case with God Consciousness. God Consciousness is everywhere, in each and every way. God Consciousness is in all time: in the present, the past, and the future. God Consciousness is unlimited by time and space.

The limited state of being is insentient (*jaḍa*), and yet the possessor of this state of insentience is completely independent

4. The moment you recognize Him in a universal way as unlimited you will also recognize Him individually as limited. This is His play. The limited insentient state of consciousness is also the Lord.

(*svatantra*), intelligent (*bodha*), and absolutely different (*vilakṣaṇa*) from that state.

So this limited "form of consciousness" is attributed only to insentience. But He has created that. For example, a rock is a creation of God when it is only a rock. But a rock is God itself when, while it is rock, it is also a human being, a god, a tree, a bird.[5]

This is His play and the reason why He has created differentiated existence. In His play He has played this kind of trick wherein the rock becomes only a rock. It is totally unaware of anything, including its true nature as universal God Consciousness. And in His play He enjoys the state of a rock being limited to being a rock and also being universal.

So there are two states to consider: the state of ignorance and the state of knowledge. When there is knowledge, a rock is not only rock, it is also universal. With knowledge, a rock is a rock and it is also all people; it is all trees, it is everything. When there is intelligence a rock is everyone and everything. But when a rock is just a rock, when it is ignorant, then it is a rock and nothing else. But at the same time, in that rock God is satisfied.

Lord Śiva enjoys the seeming limited aspect of ignorance because He knows that ignorance is not, in the real sense, ignorance at all. He enjoys that. So you cannot recognize Him in only one way. At the very moment you recognize Him in one way you will recognize Him in the other way as well. This is the reality of Kashmir Śaivism as explained by Abhinavagupta.

9. *This Lord Śiva, who is completely independent* (svatantra), *has the diversity of creation and destruction existing in His own nature. And, at the same time, this diversity is found existing in its own way as the field of ignorance.*

---

5. From the point of view of the rock, a rock is only a rock. This is the state of insentient limited being. From the point of view of Universal Consciousness, the rock is one with the Lord. From the point of view of Universal Consciousness, there is nothing that is outside of Universal Consciousness. The rock is, therefore, a human being, a god, etc., because it is one with the universal state of God Consciousness.

This is why our masters have taught us to meditate, to find out what the rock truly is. When you meditate then the rock will become universal.

When there is nothing then there is no problem. When there is only yourself then there is a problem. When there is only the other person then there is a problem. But when you come to know that you are universal then there is no problem. This is why meditation has been expounded in Śaivism, in order for you to realize the reality of God Consciousness.

Creation and destruction (*sṛiṣṭi-saṁhāra*) also take place together. In this way there is creation and destruction in the cycle of action, and creation and destruction in the cycle of knowledge. Creation and destruction in the cycle of action is just what takes place in the world of ignorance. For instance, there is a mountain. It is created and it exists in the realm of action. The results of this action are that after one thousand centuries this mountain will become dust. It will fall and crumble. This is creation and destruction in the cycle of action.

Now, you have to transform this action, the activity of this created thing, into knowledge. Then action will become universal. In that universality there is knowledge, pure knowledge (*pūrṇa-jñāna*). So, in this creation and destruction, when action is created, knowledge is destroyed, and when knowledge is created, action is destroyed.

For instance, I perceive a mountain, it is in action. It is gradually crumbling into dust. If I perceive it in knowledge, the knowledge of God Consciousness will transform this perception making it universal, and I will not feel that it is in action. The reason being that after one thousand centuries, this mountain will become dust. I will feel that it has taken the formation of dust. I will not feel that it is destroyed. So it was not in action, it was in knowledge. In universality a rock is God and dust is also God.

Knowing that there is no difference between the dust and the rock is knowledge. In the beginning the dust was rock and it had the shape of rock. After two thousand centuries the shape of the rock changed and it became dust. And yet, when there is real knowledge, there is no difference between these two, the rock and dust. That is God.

So the variation of creation and destruction take place in this way so that there is no effect at all, no effect in either way. If the variation of creation and destruction were only in action, and not in knowledge, then creation and destruction would actually take place. But whenever, after many lifetimes, real knowledge dawns, you will find out and you will recognize that from the very beginning nothing has actually happened. You were already there. Though real knowledge appeared to be destroyed, it was not destroyed. This is the trick, the play of Lord Śiva—to make knowledge appear as if it has been destroyed.

So what is the purpose of action? It is completely independent and it is play. The purpose of this action is play.

It is said,

> *At the time of reaching the superstate of God Consciousness, pleasure and pain have no value. Pleasure is the same, pain is the same, death is the same, life is the same. At that moment bondage and liberation are the same. Existence and nonexistence are the same. Becoming a rock and becoming intelligent are the same.*

In verse nine, Abhinavagupta explained that the varieties of creation and destruction are residing in Lord Śiva's own nature. Lord Śiva creates, protects, and destroys this universe. Lord Śiva also, in His own nature, conceals and reveals Himself. In the next verse he says,

> 10. *In this world you will find varieties of creation and destruction, some of which are created in the upper cycle, some of which are created below, and some of which are even created sideways. Attached to these worlds smaller portions of worlds are created. Pain, pleasure, and intellectual power are created according to the status of being. This is the world.*

You find varieties of creation and destruction in this world. And there is also variation in these varieties. Variation means that the varieties of creation and destruction do not correspond to each other. For instance, our period of twenty-four hours is the span of a mosquito's life. That is, twenty-four hours for a human is equal to one hundred years for the mosquito. Now the greatest span of a human life is one hundred years. It is said that six months to a human is equal to twenty-four hours for those gods residing in the worlds of the ancestors (*pitṛi-loka*). This is how time expands. Our six months is equal to their twenty-four hours. And this expansion of time continues all the way to Lord Śiva where the blinking of His eyes is equal to the lifetime of one hundred years of *Sadāśiva*.[6] This is the variety we come to know in this universe of one hundred and eighteen worlds.

This is variation in the varieties of creation and destruction, and these varieties are according to time. You cannot, therefore, depend upon time. Time only appears, it does not exist.

This is why Abhinavagupta, in this verse, says that in these one hundred and eighteen worlds there is an infinite variety of creation. And moreover, in this world pain, pleasure, and intellectual power are all created according to the status of being.

For example, a mosquito cannot meditate. Whereas, on the other hand, Lord Śiva can. Intellectual power, therefore, is also created with variations. A mosquito has intellectual power according to its existence and Lord Śiva has intellectual power according to His existence. And, this intellectual power is also a trick, part of Lord Śiva's play. This is the world.

11. *If you do not understand that there is actually no span of time, this misunderstanding is also the independence* (svātantrya) *of Lord Śiva. This misunderstanding results in worldly existence* (saṁsāra). *And those who are ignorant are terrified by worldly existence.*

If the notion of time were correct, then there would not be this difference of time where your one human day is equal to one hun-

6. The words "blinking of His eyes," are used just to make you understand that it is just a flash. "Blinking" is not exactly the blinking of His eye. When Lord Śiva opens His eyes Sadāśiva is created and when He closes His eyes Sadāśiva is destroyed.

dred years in the life of the mosquito. This difference of time is also the independence (*svātantrya*) of Lord Śiva. If you want to ask the question, "Why?" I will answer you by saying that you should not delve deeply into it. The "why" cannot be understood. And if it is not understood, that too is the *svātantrya* of Lord Śiva.

In this worldly existence (*saṁsāra*), ignorant people are terrified and cry out because of this independent, free will of Lord Śiva. They do not know of its existence, and they do not know that they do not know. They do not even feel that they do not know. If they did feel that they did not know, they would know. As soon as they felt that they did not know, they would know. What terrifies them is just not knowing and not knowing that they do not know. This is pure ignorance. This is that ignorance where those who are ignorant do not know that they are ignorant.

12. & 13. *When, because the grace of Lord Śiva is showered upon you, or due to the teachings or vibrating force of your Master, or through understanding the scriptures concerned with Supreme Śiva, you attain the real knowledge of reality, that is the existent state of Lord Śiva, and that is final liberation. This fullness is achieved by elevated souls and is called liberation in this life* (jīvanmukti).

Yogis understand that *saṁsāra* is only a trick, that there is actually no span of time. They know that if there were a span of time then differences of time would not exist. If time *really* existed then twenty four hours for the mosquito would be the same as it is for humans and the same as it is for Lord Śiva.

In this universe of 118 worlds all varieties of creation are in the grip of time (*kāla*), and this time is controlled by the Lord of Death (*Yama*). When there is time there is death. When there is time there is birth. When there is the kingdom of time there is everything: there is pain, there is pleasure, there is sadness, there is happiness, there is joy, there is sex, there is the absence of sex, there is detachment, and there is attachment. In this world you are caught in the grip of time to the extent of your own capacity.

Now sometimes, in some places, on some occasions it happens that the grace of Lord Śiva is showered on a person. When that grace of Lord Śiva is showered on you, or when your God Consciousness is vibrated by the vibrating force of the teachings of your master, then you come to understand that there is no time. Then you realize that a trick is being played on you by Lord Śiva. Otherwise, you will not realize that you are just like a football being played in this world. When one is filled with ignorance, he has the false understanding that he is the player. He thinks that he himself is playing. This is a false notion! He is not the player, he is the one being played.

When you come to know that this is a trick, you have nothing to do. But how do you come to know that this is a trick? You come to know by the grace of Lord Śiva; you come to know by the grace of your master; you come to know by the grace of the scriptures (*śāstras*).

If you say that you can come to know that this is a trick from lectures or from reading, I say that this is not real knowledge. It is attached knowledge. Real knowledge exists when you know yourself exactly.

14. *These two cycles, bondage and liberation, are the play of Lord Śiva and nothing else. They are not separate from Lord Śiva because differentiated states have not risen at all. In reality, nothing has happened to Lord Śiva.*

In the two cycles of bondage and liberation, the cycle of bondage is concerned with the not-knowing cycle. When you do not know what you are doing, then you do not know where you are established. That is the cycle of bondage. What is the cycle of knowledge? It is liberation! What is liberation? Liberation exists when you come to understand that it is only a trick, that it is the play of Lord Śiva and nothing else. At that point you understand that nothing has happened, nothing is lost, and nothing is gained.

In brief and exact words, these two cycles, bondage and liberation, are not separate from Lord Śiva. Why? Because differentiated states have not risen at all. It is only a trick that you are ignorant and somebody else is elevated. But the question arises—

whose trick is it? Is it your trick or Lord Śiva's trick? It is your trick. Why? Because if it were not your trick then you could not be liberated. It is your own trick that has made you ignorant. You fool yourself. And when that supreme force enters you it will shatter this ignorance into pieces. You do not need anybody's help in shattering it. You have enslaved yourself; you can free yourself and become a king.

You must understand that, in reality, nothing has happened to Lord Śiva. He is never ignorant, He is never elevated. From which point would He be elevated? Was He not elevated before? Why even use this word "elevation"? Elevation is meant for those who are sunk or who are sinking. If He has never sunk down, and you are one with Him, then why talk of elevating yourself? You are already elevated, you are divine.

This is Kashmir Śaivism. This theory of Śaivism is misunderstood by many people. You must first come to understand this theory and then you will begin to become Lord Śiva. According to the theory of Śaivism, you are Śiva, and will eventually come to the conclusion that you are Śiva. And yet, you are not actually Śiva, because you have not achieved that state.

Even though you have not actually realized that you are Śiva, it is not a mistake to think that you are Śiva. You should go on thinking that you are Śiva. You should always elevate yourself with the thought that you are Lord Śiva—but do not boast of this. If you tell someone that you are Śiva it means that you are not Lord Śiva. You must actually understand that if you are Lord Śiva, then this whole creation is all a joke, an expression of your play.

One might ask, "How do you know whether or not you are fooling yourself thinking that you are Śiva, or whether you really *are* Lord Śiva? How do you know?" The answer is that you will come to know yourself because you will be blissful, you will always be blissful. When you are in that state and when something bad happens to you, you will not get worried; and when something good happens to you, you will not get excited. While experiencing pain you will be peaceful.

You must come to know and see in yourself situated in this way. If you are not situated in this way and boast, saying, "I am

Lord Śiva, I am Lord Śiva," you will be slapped and made to understand that you are not Lord Śiva.

To actually know who you are is a big problem. You have to find out yourself where you are situated. It happens by the grace of Lord Śiva, or by the grace of a master, or by the grace of the *śāstras.*

15. *In this way the Lord, Bhairava, the essence of all being, has held in His own way in His own nature, the three great energies: the energy of will* (icchā-śakti), *the energy of action* (kriyā-śakti), *and the energy of knowledge* (jñāna-śakti). *These three energies are just like that trident*[7] *which is the three-fold lotus. And seated on this lotus is Lord Bhairava, who is the nature of the whole universe of 118 worlds.*

The nature of the universe is the existence of Lord Śiva. Lord Śiva's existence is naturally everyone's nature. Lord Śiva is found in rocks; Lord Śiva is found everywhere. Lord Śiva is even found in the absence of Lord Śiva. Even there He is not absent, He is existing.

There He resides, alone in His kingdom. No one else is found there.

16. *I, Abhinavagupta, have written and revealed these verses for some of my dear disciples who have very little intellectual understanding. For those disciples, who are deeply devoted to me, I have composed these fifteen verses just to elevate them instantaneously.*

7. The *triśula* is a trident carried by ascetics, a symbol of Lord Śiva.

TWO

Talks on Practice

1. First Talk

This is a discourse on the ways which, if followed, and adhered to, will lead an aspirant (*sādhaka*) to one-pointedness in meditation and to the awareness to which he aspires. The first requirement for achievement of this goal is that the mind (*manas*) be absolutely clean. A "clean mind" is one that knows no duality, a mind that has feelings of sameness for everyone. This "sameness," known as *samabhāva,* means that you do not overexpress or underexpress love for any one person in particular.

Furthermore, to reach this state you should not have animosity (*vairabhāva*) toward any person. If you do not have the feeling of sameness towards everyone, and if you do not shun feelings of animosity towards everyone, then all your efforts to achieve the Truth and the Absolute in meditation will be totally wasted. All your efforts will go unrewarded like carrying water in a wicker basket.

In meditation there is no room for coarse feelings. The mind must be absolutely clean and purged of all acts of hate and feigned love. Both are evils. Only when the mind has been purged of these two acts can you meditate with confidence. At that point you will be glorified by the fruits of divine meditation.

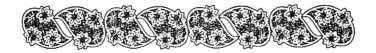

Now I shall explain to you how to enter this realm of meditation. When you have decided to meditate, the first thing that must be attended to is the seat (*āsana*), the place where you choose to sit for meditation. On this seat you must sit still without your body moving. It is best to remain absolutely motionless like a rock. You should not twitch your eyelids, move your lips, or scratch your ears or nose. You should be like a frozen body, absolutely motionless.

It matters little if, when you are first settling into your *āsana*, thoughts continue to stream through your mind. At this point you should simply avoid physical distractions such as moaning and sneezing. After an hour you will feel that your mind has begun settling into a subtle state of thought and mood. Gradually you will experience that your mind is moving into the domain of meditation, which is filled with peace and rest. Here your mind will become one-pointed (*ekāgra*) and subtle (*sūkṣma*).

In the *Bhagavad Gītā* the Lord says:

> *As the wandering mind will never remain on one point, you must be ever vigilant; whenever it strays, bring it under control and fix it again towards God Consciousness.*[1]
>
> Bhagavad Gītā 6:27

You need not struggle to fix your mind upon that point from which it has begun to waiver. In the initial stage of your exercise you only need to sit still with one-pointed effort (*ekāgra*). In one hour you will understand and experience, through one-pointedness, the bliss of the dawning of Awareness. As it is further stated in the *Bhagavad Gītā*:

> *You must sit erect for meditation with enough strength to maintain that position and, at the same time, you must fix your gaze in the direction of the tip of your nose in order to restrain your eyes from wandering.*[2]
>
> Bhagavad Gītā 6:14

---

1. yato yato niścarati manaś cañcalam asthiram /
   tatas tato niyamyaitad ātmany eva śamaṁ nayet //
2. samaṁ kāyaśirogrīvaṁ dhārayann acalaṁ sthiraḥ /
   saṁpaśyan·nāsikāgraṁ svaṁ diśaś cānavalokayan //

The posture has to be quite steady, straight, and motionless; one-pointed, with the mind fully concentrated on the *guru-śabda* or *guru-dhāraṇā*. Though the literal meaning of the text is that the aspirant should direct his sight in the direction of his nose (*nāsikāgram*), it may also be taken to refer to concentration on the word of the master (*guru-śabda*) or the resonance of unlimited I-Consciousness (*guru-dhāraṇā*), which the *guru* embodies and which is to be found in the junction (*sandhi*). This state of concentration can be achieved only after you have freed your mind of all worldly cares, completed your daily routine activities, and have had your full amount of sleep. Your mind must be absolutely free from all preoccupations. Then alone will you be able to meditate without deviation and gaze within yourself.

In the *Bhagavad Gītā* the Lord says:

> *At the time of meditation your mind must be serene, free from the forced obligation to meditate, determined with devotion to discover God Consciousness. In this state your mind is to be continuously directed toward God Consciousness.*[3]
>
> Bhagavad Gītā 6:15

In this verse the Lord is telling us that a seeker must be serene, fearless, and determined in order to achieve his goal. He should be subdued in mind, at harmony, and in peace. With devotion you should meditate with vigor. There should be no outside pressure which forces you to meditate. It should be an outflowing of your own desire. In this verse, the words *brahmacāri-vrata* mean full of devotion and determination in thought; it does not mean that you have to embellish yourself with a saffron robe or keep a long tuft of hair on your head and a large religious mark on your forehead. It doesn't mean you must wear a garland and cover your

3. praśāntātmā vigatabhīr brahmacārivrate sthitaḥ /
manaḥ saṁyamya maccitto yukta āsīta matparaḥ //

body and forehead with ash. Here the Lord is only describing the physical posture (*āsana*) needed for meditation. There is also an internal posture (*āntarika āsana*) which enables the mind to be one-pointed towards and in Awareness.

> *On the pathway of your breath, maintain continuously refreshed and full awareness on, and in the center of, the breathing in and breathing out. This is force and this is internal* āsana.[4]
>
> Netra Tantra 8:11

Your concentration has to be on the center. You must practice on the junction (Sanskrit: *sandhi*). You must concentrate on the word of the master (*guru-śabda*) with full devotion and be aware of the center of the inhaling and exhaling of the breath. You should not only concentrate on the center when the center is reached at the end point of exhaling; but from the beginning of the breath until the end point of exhaling. The effort is to be one-pointed in the center. You must meditate in this way for your efforts not to be wasted.

Exhaling and inhaling also refer to day and night. That is, the best time to practice meditation is not during the day or during the night, but in the center between the two, in the morning when the goddess of the dawn meets the day, and in the evening, when the dusk meets the night, when the sun seems to sink into the horizon. I swear by Absolute Reality that if you practice meditation in this way you will never fail.

There can be no one-pointedness of continuously fresh awareness (*anusandhānaikāgratā*) in absolute day or absolute night. Even if you remain conscious while exhaling and inhaling you will achieve nothing.

---

4. madhyamaṁ prāṇamāśritya
prāṇāpānapathāntaram /
ālambhya jñānaśaktiṁ ca
tatsthaṁ caivāsanaṁ labhet //

Do not worship the Lord during the day. Do not worship the Lord during the night. The Lord must be worshipped at the point of the meeting of day and night.[5]

Quoted in Tantrāloka 6

Do not worship God during the day or the night; do not meditate during the day or the night; do not maintain awareness upon exhaling (day) or inhaling (night). Concentrate on the center. The Lord of gods must be worshipped where day and night meet. This is meditating on the junction (*sandhi*).

When my master first told me about this meditation I immediately began practicing it. I started hurriedly and abruptly without understanding this meditation completely. Sometimes when I tell one of my devotees to go and do something for me he immediately runs off to accomplish what I have ordered him to do without understanding what I really want. In his excitement he simply rushes to do it. So in the same way when my *guru* said that I must meditate at these times, I immediately rushed off to begin. I did not wait to ask my master the means and method for doing it. I just began practicing. I exhaled and inhaled but nothing happened. I became dismayed. I cried in my failure. I felt so sad for not having achieved anything.

Once while feeling quite disappointed I became drowsy and quickly fell asleep. I had a dream in which I thought, "Let me go to the *ashram* to seek the guidance of my master." And in this dream I went to the *ashram*. But at the *ashram* I didn't see my master, I saw my grandmaster, Swami Ram. I appealed to him saying "Sir, I feel as if I am achieving nothing. My efforts are going to waste." My grandmaster told me, "You should practice *sand* (the junction)." Then my dream abruptly ended and I opened my eyes.

The next day I went to my master and told Him about my dream. I told him that I wanted to know the meaning of the words, "You should practice *sand*." My master said, "Yes, you started to

5. na divā pūjayeddevaṁ
rātrau naiva ca naiva ca /
arcayeddevadeveśaṁ
dinarātriparikṣaye //

practice in a hurry and in haste without proper understanding. Before beginning you have to learn this practice properly."

In the Kashmiri language the word *sand* is used for the Sanskrit word *sandhi*. *Sand* means meditation, and maintaining awareness is not an ordinary affair. You have to be aware at the door of the *Brahmapurī*, the center of the two breaths.

> *If you meditate upon your Self ceaselessly, remaining always attached to Me, thinking of Me alone, you will gain that peace which is residing in My own nature and which will effortlessly carry you to liberation.*[6]
>
> Bhagavad Gītā 6:16

You must have full faith and complete attachment to meditation. It must not become a routine or a chore. When you are about to meditate you must feel excitement (*harṣa*) and be thankful to God that you have received this opportunity of beginning meditation (*abhyāsa*). Unless you fall in love with meditation and approach it with total enthusiasm, attachment, and longing, you cannot enter the realm of Awareness. All your efforts to achieve Awareness are likely to fail. They will be useless and futile.

The aspirant who is dedicated to this glorified state of Awareness, and maintains peace and harmony, will attain that *nirvāṇa* which abides in the Kingdom of the Lord.

You must unravel all the various knots that exist in your mind. For example, if you are feeling jealousy, thinking that the *guru* is concerned with another disciple more than you, then you are not thinking properly. You should not think this way. You must concentrate on your *guru* and not on your *guru*-brother. Thoughts of this kind are full of avarice and jealousy. Through these thoughts you deviate and wander adrift in the desert. You should not look to see whom your *guru* is looking at. Keeping your mind absolutely pure you should concentrate on your *guru* alone.

Now I shall tell you about the nature of *āsana* (seat). Although the word *āsana* generally means the erect posture assumed in meditation, this is not its central or essential meaning. When I use the word *āsana* I do not mean the various forms of *āsana*

---

6. yuñjann evaṁ sadātmānaṁ madbhakto 'nanyamānasaḥ /
śāṁtiṁ nirvāṇaparamāṁ matsaṁsthām adhigacchati //

such as the lotus posture (*padma āsana*), etc. By '*āsana*' I mean something else. First let me speak to you about breath, about the inhaling breath (*apāna*) and the exhaling breath (*prāṇa*). Breath is extremely important in meditation, particularly the central breath (*madhyamaṁ prāṇam*). This central breath is neither the exhaling breath nor the inhaling breath. It is the center of these two, the point existing between the inhalation and exhalation. This central point cannot be held by any physical means like a material object can be held by the hand. The center between the two breaths can be held only by knowledge, *jñāna*. This knowledge is not discursive knowledge, it is that knowledge which is pure awareness. When this central point is held with continuously refreshed awareness (*anusandhāna*)—which is knowledge, and which is achieved through devotion (*bhakti*) to the Lord—this is, in the true sense, settling into your *āsana*. *Āsana*, therefore, is the gradual dawning of the Awareness which shines in the central point between inhalation and exhalation.

This Awareness is not gained by a person who is full of prejudice, avarice, or envy. Such a person, being filled with negative qualities, cannot concentrate. The prerequisite of this glorious achievement is, therefore, the purification of your internal sense of self. It must become pure, clean, and crystal clear. After you have purged your mind of all prejudice and have started settling with full awareness into that point between the two breaths, then you are settling into your *āsana*.

> *If when breathing in and breathing out you maintain a continual awareness on the center between the incoming and outgoing breath, then your breath will spontaneously and progressively become more refined. At that point you are elevated to another world. That is* prāṇāyāma.[7]
>
> Netra Tantra 8:12–13

---

7. prāṇādisthūlabhāvaṁ tu
tyaktvā sūkṣmamathāntaram /
sūkṣmātītaṁ tu paramaṁ
spandanaṁ labhyate yataḥ //
prāṇāyāmaḥ sa nirddiṣṭo
yasmānna cyavate punaḥ //

After assuming the *āsana* of meditation, the refined practice of *prāṇāyāma* arises. *Prāṇāyāma* is not vigorously inhaling and exhaling like a bellows. Like *āsana, prāṇāyāma* is internal and very subtle. There is an uninterrupted continuity in moving your awareness from the point of *āsana* into the practice of *prāṇāyāma.* When, through your awareness, you have settled in your *āsana,* then you automatically enter into the practice of *prāṇāyāma.*

Our masters have indicated that there are two principle forms of this practice of *āsana-prāṇāyāma*, called *cakrodaya* and *ajapā-gāyatrī.* In the practice of *ajapā-gāyatrī,* you must maintain continuously refreshed full awareness in the center of the two breaths. This is done while breathing in and out, slowly and silently, without sound. Likewise, in the practice of *cakrodaya,* you must maintain awareness that is continually fresh, new, and filled with excitement and vigor in the center of the two breaths. You breathe in and breathe out slowly, but in this case you breathe in and breathe out while creating sound with the breath.

Ajapā-gāyatrī is therefore continually refreshed awareness (*anusandhāna*) combined with the slow and silent movement of the breath. The inhaling and exhaling should be so slow and so utterly silent that even the one who is breathing will not be able to hear his own breath. To illustrate this form of *prāṇāyāma* the Kashmiri saint Paramānanda said,

> *You must ascend that mountain known as Pañcāla. This mountain, composed of the glory of God Consciousness, is the mountain of Bhairava filled with the* mantra so'ham. *This ascent, which begins after your mind is established in God Consciousness, must be accomplished very slowly so that the jewel which is your goal, and which lies on the peak of this mountain, is preserved and not destroyed.*[8]

---

8. ast ast khast pañcālasīy
so'haṁ bhairavabhālāsiy /
ṭokh yuthna ati lagi lālasiy
mana sthira kara pūjona prabhu //

Your awareness during this ascent must be strong and fresh and held in continuity. You must maintain an undisturbed movement of the breath. It should be slow, inaudible, and without break or pause. The continuity of this movement is extremely important, and it must be maintained with complete awareness focused in between the two breaths. You must maintain full awareness at the point where the inhaling breath reaches its completion, the place where the exhaling breath is born. You must also maintain awareness at the end point of exhalation, the place where the inhaling breath is born. The practice of *ajapā-gāyatrī* does not allow for the missing of a single breath. Your awareness must be unbroken. It must be unbroken, continuously refreshed, and fixed in the center of the two slowly and silently moving breaths. This is *ajapā-gāyatrī-anusandhāna.*

The second form of the practice of *āsana-prāṇāyāma* is *cakrodaya.*

> *This* cakrodaya, *which I have described according to my own experience, the teachings of my master, and the explanation of the scriptures, must be undertaken with the most refined awareness.*[9]
>
> Tantrāloka 7:71

You must maintain the awareness which is the most subtle awareness. This is neither external awareness nor internal awareness, but that awareness that is in the center of the depths of these two. This is the meaning of the words "the most refined awareness."

There is a difference between *cakrodaya* and *ajapā-gāyatrī.* If, in the beginning, you attempt to practice *ajapā-gāyatrī,* you will fail and subsequently fall. You will only fall asleep during meditation. The practice of *ajapā-gāyatrī* is very difficult. Therefore, in the beginning, you should practice *cakrodaya.* In the final stages you can practice *ajapā-gāyatrī.* To practice *ajapā-gāyatrī* you should

9. ityeṣa sūkṣmaparimarśanaśīlanīya-
ścakrodayo'nubhavaśāstraḍriśā mayoktaḥ //

> *Ball your fists, clench your teeth, and tense all the muscles of your body, but conquer your mind.*[10]
>
> Yogavāsiṣṭhasāra

This is the advice of Vasiṣṭha to Rāma. He tells him that he must first conquer his mind. Unless you have courage you cannot conquer your mind, and unless you have conquered your mind you cannot dare to practice *ajapā-gāyatrī.*

In *cakrodaya* there exists the gross movement of breath. It is breath with sound. Through practice, this gross movement of breath is refined and, with the passage of time, becomes more and more subtle. This can only be accomplished through one's own will and concentration. Even the *guru*'s grace (*guru-kṛipā*) will not help a seeker unless he is determined and fully devoted to maintaining awareness and concentration. This grace of the *guru* helps those who are simple, and simple are those who have awareness and consciousness. The spiritual aspirant who waivers and becomes disturbed gains nothing.

If you undergo these practices for one thousand centuries without full awareness and concentration you will have wasted all one thousand of those centuries. The movement of breath has to be filled with full awareness and concentration.

> *God Consciousness is not achieved by means of the scriptures nor is it achieved by the grace of your master. God Consciousness is only achieved by your own subtle awareness.*[11]
>
> Yogavāsiṣṭha

---

10. hastaṁ hastena saṁpīḍya
dantairdantāṁśca pīḍayan /
aṅgānyaṅgairsamākramya
jayedādau svakaṁ manaḥ //

11. na śāstrair nāpi guruṇā
dṛiśyate parameśvaraḥ /
dṛiśyate svātmanaivātmā
svayā sattvasthayā dhiyā //

The scriptures will not lift a seeker nor can his master elevate him, but when his consciousness is fixed in his own awareness then his soul becomes visible.

By maintaining the constantly refreshed continuity of your awareness in the center of the two breaths (*madhyamaṁ prāṇam*) through the practice of either *ajapā-gāyatrī* or *cakrodaya,* you settle in your *āsana* and *prāṇāyāma* commences. The movement of your breath becomes very subtle, very refined, as if thin. At this stage you feel like going to sleep, but it is not really sleep. You are proceeding towards the subtle state of awareness (*sūkṣma-gati*). Your awareness will not allow you to fall asleep. At this point you enter the fourth state (*turya*) which is neither the waking state (*jāgrat*), the dreaming state (*svapna*), nor the deep sleep state (*suṣupti*). This is the beginning of *parama-spanda-tattva*. About this Śaṅkarācārya has said,

> *If you maintain your awareness at that point which is found between waking and sleeping, you will be focused on that supreme felicity which is the supreme bliss of God Consciousness.*[12]
>
> Ślokāṣṭaka

This is that point, which is found at the ending of wakefulness and the beginning of sleep, the point between waking and sleeping. This junction is very important, it is the entrance into the state of *turya*, which has opened as a result of settling into your *āsana* and undergoing *prāṇāyāma.*

Long ago I composed these lines:

There is a point between sleep and waking
Where you must remain alert without shaking.
Enter into the new world
Where hideous forms will pass.

---

12. yadbhāvānubhavaḥ syān-
nidrādau jāgarasyānte /
antaḥ sa cet sitharaḥ
syāllabhate tadadvayānandam //

They are passing. Endure.
Do not be taken by the dross.
Then the pulls and pushes about the throttle,
all those you must tolerate.
Close all ingress and egress.
Yawnings there may be.
Shed tears, crave, implore,
and you will not prostrate.
A thrill passes and that goes down to the bottom.
It rises—may it bloom forth.
That is Bliss.
Blessed Being! Blessed Being!
O greetings be to Thee! [13]

---

13. In these verses Swami Lakshmanjoo reveals his experience of the dawning and unfolding of that supreme mystical experience known as *kuṇḍalinī*. Here Swamiji tells us that the journey of rising begins when the seeker maintains his awareness in continuity by concentrating on the center and enters the junction, the gap, found between sleep and waking. Here you must remain alert. You must not fall asleep. Then you will begin to experience the death of your limited self in preparation for the awakening of your universal Self. This experience may be horrible and terrifying. You may actually experience that you are dying or that the house you're in is burning. You must not be fainthearted and give up. If you do you will pull yourself out of your meditation trance. Instead you must be firm and fast in your dedication and devotion to your goal. You must long and hunger for this highest realization. If you continue in this manner, then your incoming and outgoing breath will stop and your breath will whirl about one point. If you maintain your awareness, then your breath is transformed from *prāṇa* (breath) into *prāṇana* (life), and it is sipped down through the central vein, which lies on the right side of the passage of the breath, to a place near the rectum known as *mūlādhāra*. It is said to be "sipped down" because during this process you actually experience a sipping sound. In *mūlādhāra* you experience a crawling sensation which is like the experience when sexual climax is just about to take place. After a momentary experience of this sensation your *kuṇḍalinī,* which is that internal serpent power residing in *mūlādhāra* in the shape of a coil, rises in one flash. When it rises you become filled with absolutely blissful existence. The happiness and bliss that you experience cannot be described. Here you attain that supreme state of the bliss of Enlightenment and recognize the reality of the Self.

2. Second Talk

I have explained that there are two means for settling into your *āsana* and practicing *prāṇāyāma, ajapā-gāyatrī-anusandhāna* and *cakrodaya anusandhāna*. Here the word *āsana* means maintaining full, ever-refreshed awareness on and in the center of the two breaths (*madhyamaṁ prāṇam*). The spontaneous refinement of the breath (*prāṇāyāma*) results through the settling into your *āsana* and brings about entry into the fourth state (*turya*).

Previously I suggested, because of the difficutly in practicing *ajapā-gāyatrī*, that you begin with the practice of *cakrodaya*. In this practice you must inhale and exhale in long breaths with sound. Long breaths do not occupy as much space in the movement of breath. Inhaling and exhaling quickly, in short breaths, occupies much more space. The longer the breath, the less space it occupies; the less space it occupies, the quicker the results. Kallaṭa has said,

> *By decreasing the span of your breathing by just one* tuṭi *you will become omniscient and omnipotent.*[14]

The movement of the breath occupies sixteen *tuṭis* from its internal beginning point at the heart to its external ending point. One *tuṭi* is equivalent to the space occupied by two and a quarter fingers laid side by side. At certain times the breath may occupy seventeen *tuṭis*. When for example you are very afraid and running very fast, the breath occupies more space.

In the practice of *cakrodaya* the breath must occupy a minimum amount of space. At the time of practice you must be able to hear the sound of the inhaling and exhaling breath. The sound of your breathing should be loud enough for those sitting near you to hear it.

There are two different views of how to practice *cakrodaya*. Some say that the breath should be inhaled and exhaled by the

---

14. tuṭipāte sarvajñatvasarvakartṛitvalābhaḥ.

throat. Others say that the breath should be inhaled and exhaled by the heart. Those who say that the breath should be inhaled and exhaled by the heart are wrong. This is a very dangerous and deadly procedure. This practice will produce such powerful and intense heat that the heart will be adversely effected and damaged. You could die within the span of a few weeks. Therefore, *cakrodaya* must be practiced by inhaling and exhaling by the throat, not by the heart.

Through the practice of *cakrodaya*, your *āsana* is established and your breath (*prāṇa*) becomes more refined, more subtle. At this point begins *prāṇāyāma,* and you gain entry into the fourth state (*turya*) automatically. This fourth state (*turya*), which is neither wakefulness (*jāgrat*), dreaming (*svapna*), nor deep sleep (*suṣupti*), exists in the junction between any of these three states: between waking and dreaming, dreaming and deep sleep, and deep sleep and waking.

Now your breath, though extremely subtle and refined, continues to move in and out. Your awareness is full. You do not feel giddy or lazy. These feelings pass the moment you gain entry into *turya.* In your spiritual journey you are now at the point when *prāṇāyāma* moves towards *pratyāhāra*. Here action (*karma*) does not exist for you. The organs of action (*karmendriyas*) become powerless. You cannot move your hands or fingers; nor can you move your legs or feet, open your eyes, or even wink. From the point of view of action and activity you can do nothing. You hear external sounds but only indistinctly. They don't capture your attention. You don't become involved in them. They appear to you as a far-off whisper.

> *When walking on a path you perceive all the features of the landscape, grass, trees, clouds; but they don't leave impressions in your mind. In this manner you must act in the world. Do everything but leave the impressions behind.*[15]

When you are walking, you do not notice the falling of the leaves or the movements of the clouds in the sky. In the same way, the spiritual seeker who has entered *turya* is not concerned

15. rathyāṁ gamane tṛiṇaparaṇādivat

with external events occurring around him. This is the full state of *prāṇāyāma*. The external journey in waking, dreaming, and deep sleep has ended, and the internal journey in the fourth state has begun.

This internal voyage will be long and arduous. I advise you, therefore, not to envy your spiritual brother or sister. Be without avarice and hate. This path is tortuous like the path of a maze or a labyrinth. Concentrate on your journey alone. Do not find fault or concern yourself with others. Love is the answer and the key. Through love you can find the way through this maze. This is a very difficult journey, and the goal is not easily attained.

> *Saints and wise men of old have taught that travelling on the path of spirituality is very difficult. It is like walking on the edge of an extremely sharp sword.*[16]
>
> Kaṭha Upaniṣad 1:3.14

At the beginning of this internal journey, in the state of *prāṇāyāma*, you will vividly experience the five subtle elements (*tanmātrās*): subtle hearing (*śabda*), subtle touch (*sparśa*), subtle sight (*rūpa*), subtle taste (*rasa*), and subtle smell (*gandha*). As you are breathing slowly in and out with full awareness, as your master has instructed you, these elements attack your five senses, and you perceive them vividly and clearly. The experience of these five subtle elements is irresistible and filled with sensual enjoyment. It surpasses the experience of the most wonderful sound, the most enjoyable touch, the most lovely sight, the most delicious taste, and the most fragrant smell. Being that these experiences are so attractive, they are extremely distracting. But you must not be distracted by these experiences. You must continue on your journey toward *pratyāhāra*.

Beloved Śaṅkara has said,

> *When, during meditation, you experience the divinely produced, internal, subtle elements, pass through them, "unminding" your mind with great awareness, and*

---

16. kṣurasya dhārā niśitā duratyayā
durgaṁ pathas tat kavayo vadanti.

enter into the supreme state of God Consciousness. This is pratyāhāra.[17]

Netra Tantra 18:13–14

In the state of *turya* you mentally perceive the presence of the five subtle elements (*tanmātrās*), but you must not indulge in these five attractions. You must completely ignore them and settle ever more deeply into your own one-pointed awareness. This settling is called *pratyāhāra*. It is the winding up of the external world and the entering into the supreme internal world. No darkness exists there. It is light itself.

Your breath is moving towards *pratyāhāra*. With vigor you must try to gain entry into that supreme state of meditation. You cannot enter it by physical force, only by the power of the mind.

Pratyāhāra *cuts the bondage of* saṁsāra.[18]

Netra Tantra 8:14

There you will find your intellect filled with ultimate truth.[19]

Yoga Sūtra 1:48

In *pratyāhāra* the intellect (*buddhi*) is filled with Truth (*ṛitaṁbharā*). Whatever is untrue cannot exist there. There you will find only Truth and Light.

Your journey in *turya* continues. Up to this point your breath is moving in meditation (*abhyāsa*). Now your breath ends and your journey to liberation turns toward contemplation (*dhyāna*).

When you pass the internal, divine sensual field you must focus your mind on that supreme all-pervading

---

17. prāṇāyamaḥ sa uddiṣṭto
 yasmānna cyavate punaḥ /
 śabdādiguṇavṛitiryā
 cetasā hyanubhūyate //
 tyaktvā tāṁ praviśeddhāma
 paramaṁ tatsvacetasā /
 pratyāhāraḥ iti proktaḥ
18. bhavapāśanikṛintakaḥ
19. ṛitaṁbharā tatra prajñā //

God Consciousness. Then, spontaneously, Supreme God Consciousness will shine before you. This is contemplation (dhyāna).[20]

Netra Tantra 8:15

Earlier I told you that when you enter into the state of "I" the five organs of action (*karmendriyas*) become powerless. They cease to function. Upon gaining entry into the state of *pratyāhāra,* the five subtle elements (*tanmātrās*) are eliminated. The breath is also annihilated when it enters into the central channel (*suṣumnā-nāḍī*). At this point your journey of meditation ends. This state cannot be concentrated upon; it is held automatically.

In this regard there is an ancient teaching in Kashmir that has been passed by word of mouth from generation to generation,

Let me have the power to do where there is nothing to be done. Let me have the power to contemplate where there is nothing to contemplate.

When the breath enters the *suṣumnā-nāḍī,* this is the beginning of the journey of contemplation (*dhyāna*).

When the yogī *confirms internally that he will do whatever the state of God Consciousness wills, and when he takes hold of spanda-tattva, his breath enters the central channel and rises again in the* ūrdhva-mārga *as* kuṇḍalinī. *Here also, he must remain alert and aware or he will enter the state of sleep.*[21]

Spanda Kārikā 1:23–24

---

20. dhīguṇānsamatikramya
nirdheyaṁ paramaṁ vibhum /
dhyātvā dhyeyaṁ svasaṁvedyaṁ
dhyānaṁ tacca vidurbudhāḥ //

21. yāmavasthāṁ samālambya
yadayaṁ mama vakṣyati /
tadavaśyaṁ kariṣye'ha-
miti saṁkalpya tiṣṭhati //
tāmāśrityordhvamārgeṇa
somasūryāvubhāvapi /
sauṣuptapadavanmūḍhaḥ
prabuddhaḥ syādanāvṛitaḥ //

Here the small self, the limited ego, has been subdued. The state of breathing—inhaling and exhaling—enters into, and becomes, the state of breath itself (*prāṇana*). The seeker becomes the embodiment of the breath (*prāṇana*). His blood circulates so slowly that doctors cannot detect a pulse. At this point his body is charged as if by the shock of electric current. But the shock that the seeker experiences at this stage is not charged with fear and death but with bliss and joy. Seekers may experience this breath in different ways and, therefore, you must be aware and cautious so that you are not misled. Don't compare your experience with that of others.

In the *Tantrāloka* it states that if the master is elevated, and if the disciple is endowed with complete qualifications, then the master can assist his disciple. But on the other hand, if his disciple is not really qualified, then the master cannot properly help or elevate him.

The shock of bliss and joy experienced by the seeker is called the initiation of piercing (*vedha-dīkṣā*). This initiation is just like drilling a hole in an object. The experience of this blissful shock is one form of realization and it is one of the phases passed through on the path to liberation. This phase is called pervasion of the Self (*ātma-vyāpti*).

Our masters have taught us that the seeker can experience this joyous shock of bliss as six different qualities of piercing (*vedha*): *śakti-vedha, bindu-vedha, bhujaṅga-vedha, bhramara-vedha, nāda-vedha*, and *mantra-vedha*. All these piercings reside in the supreme movement of breath known as *prāṇa-kuṇḍalinī*.

The piercing by the blissful force of breath is experienced as energy in *śakti-vedha*. In *bindu-vedha* it is experienced as sexual bliss. If the pleasure experienced by a couple at the climax of their lovemaking is multiplied a million times, even this pleasure would not match the bliss felt by one who experiences *bindu-vedha*. In *bhujaṅga-vedha* this piercing is experienced as the rising of a cobra; in *bhramara-vedha* it is experienced as the buzzing of a black bee. In *nāda-vedha* it is experienced as sound. In *mantra-vedha* it is experienced as the knowledge of the *mantra* *"aham"* (I). In the journey to liberation the movement of *dhyāna* exists in these six *vedhas*.

There is also a seventh supreme *vedha*. This *vedha*, known as *parā-vedha*, does not exist in *dhyāna*. This piercing resides in the supreme awakening known as *cit-kuṇḍalinī*. Here a seeker resides in the state of complete God Consciousness.

> *When you establish your mind in the internal reality of God Consciousness, that is* dhāraṇā. *This* dhāraṇā *is not only to be established in internal God Consciousness but also in all the activities of your worldly life. This is true* dhāraṇā.[22]
>
> Netra Tantra 8:16

Now, with the completion of the initiation of piercing, begins the journey of *dhāraṇa*. This initiation propels you on the journey of *dhāraṇā*, the journey of adjustment. Your consciousness becomes filled and adjusted with the reality and truth that this whole universe is only God. Nothing is experienced as being outside of God. This is the unification of your individual God Consciousness with Universal God Consciousness.

At this point the organs of action are again infused with power. They are reactivated. Your breath heaves and you move out into external experience; yet, while moving out, you remain in the *turya* state. The action of moving out into experience while remaining in the *turya* state is known as *krama-mudrā*. You begin to experience the state of Universal God Consciousness. You will only experience this, however, if you remain filled with active awareness.

This unification of individual God Consciousness and Universal God Consciousness leads to that supreme state where God Consciousness is experienced without break in all the states of waking, dreaming, and deep sleep. This is the supreme state of fullness while in the body and is called *jagad-ānanda*.

---

22. dhāraṇā paramātmatvaṁ
dhāryate yena sarvadā /
dhāraṇā sā vinirddiṣṭā
bhavabandhavināśinī //

THREE

Entrance into the Supreme Reality

THESE TEACHINGS ARE BASED ON THE *Parāprāveśikā* of Kṣemarāja, the chief disciple of Abhinavagupta. The word *parāprāveśikā* means "that which causes you to enter the Supreme," that which gives you a push into that highest reality.

> *I bow to that Consciousness* (saṁvid) *which shines in the three-fold ways of its energies—supreme, medium, and inferior—and in all the three states of Consciousness. That Consciousness is the heart of Lord Śiva.*

The supreme Energy (*śakti*) is that Energy beyond limitation. It is non-dual (*advaita*), monistic. Medium (*parāparā*) energy is both non-dual (*advaita*) and dual (*dvaita*). Inferior (*aparā*) energy is only dual (*dvaita*). These three energies correspond to subjective consciousness, conceptual consciousness, and objective consciousness.[1] I bow to that Consciousness which shines in these

1. These three states of consciousness are the three aspects that make up any perception. There is the perceiver, which is subjective consciousness; the means of perceiving that object, which is cognitive consciousness; and the object being perceived, which is objective consciousness.

three ways. That Consciousness is the heart of Lord Śiva. It is both one with the universe and above the universe.

Now the essence.

In the world of Śaivite philosophy Lord Śiva is seen as being filled with light. But more than this, Lord Śiva is the embodiment of light and this light is different than the light of the sun, of the moon, or of fire.

It is light (*prakaśa*) with Consciousness (*vimarśa*); and this light with Consciousness is the nature of that Supreme Consciousness, Lord Śiva.

What is Consciousness? The light of Consciousness is not only pure Consciousness, it is filled with the understanding that I am the creator, I am the protector, and I am the destroyer of everything. Just to know that I am the creator, I am the protector, and I am the destroyer is Consciousness. If Consciousness was not attached to the light of Consciousness, we would have to admit that the light of the sun or the light of the moon or the light of a fire is also Lord Śiva. But this is not the case.

The light of Consciousness (*vimarśa*) is given various names. It is called *cit-caitanya*, which means the strength of consciousness; *parā vāk,* the supreme word; *svātantrya*, perfect independence; *aiśvarya,* the predominant glory of supreme Śiva; *kartṛitva,* the power of acting; *sphurattā*, the power of existing; *sāra*, the complete essence of everything; *hṛidaya,* the universal heart; and *spanda*, universal movement. All these are names in the Tantras, which are attributed to this Consciousness.

This I-Consciousness, which is the reality of Lord Śiva, is a natural (*akṛitrima*), not a contrived, "I." It is not adjusted I-Consciousness. Limited human beings have adjusted I-Consciousness. Lord Śiva has natural or pure I-Consciousness. There is a difference between adjusted Consciousness and natural Consciousness. Adjusted or artificial Consciousness exists when this I-Consciousness is attributed to your body, to your mind, to your intellect, and to your ego. Natural Consciousness is that consciousness that is attributed to the reality of the Self, which is all Consciousness.

Natural Consciousness is the pure embodiment of Consciousness. It is Śiva. All of the thirty-six elements, from Śiva to earth, are created by that natural I-Consciousness. And not only are they created by that Consciousness, they also shine in that Consciousness. His creation is not outside of His nature, it exists in His own Self. He has created this whole universe in the cycle of His Consciousness. So, everything that exists resides in that Consciousness.

This must be your understanding. The creative energy which is attributed to Lord Śiva is not that energy of Lord Śiva that creates the universe outside of His Consciousness as we create outside of our consciousness. His creation is not insentient (*jaḍa*) as our creations are.

This universe, which is created in His Consciousness, is dependent on that Consciousness. It is always dependent on that Consciousness. It cannot move outside of that Consciousness. It exists only when it is residing in His Consciousness. This is the way the creation of His universe takes place.

You must understand that this universe, which is created by the Lord of Consciousness, is one with that Creator Who is wholly *prakāśa-vimarśa,* self-luminous light with Consciousness.

If this created universe were to remain outside of Consciousness then it would not appear to anyone. It would not exist, just as the son born of a barren woman or the milk of a bird do not exist. If we go in the depth of this understanding, we will see that there is a difference between these analogies. If this created universe were to remain outside of Consciousness, it would not appear to anyone because it would not exist at all. Actually only Consciousness exists. In this way, because this universe exists, it is one with Consciousness. In reality, nothing would exist if it were separate from this Consciousness. It is in this sense that we can say that the son of a barren woman or the milk of a bird are existing. They are existing because they are existing in Consciousness as long as they are residing in our thought. When it is in imagination it is existing in Consciousness. Kṣemarāja is telling us that this universe is not outside of Consciousness. So, the son of a barren woman or the milk of a bird are not existing outside of Consciousness. We can think of them, so they are also existing inside of Consciousness.

The Consciousness of Lord Śiva is not overshadowed by this created world. The world cannot obscure Consciousness. On the contrary, Consciousness gives rise to the existence of this world.

This world is existing on the surface of Consciousnes. So how could this world cover or conceal the nature of Consciousness? The truth is, this world gets its life from Consciousness. It is filled with the light of Consciousness. The universe can not conceal its life, which is Consciousness. If this universe could conceal the Consciousness of Lord Śiva, how would it exist? It would not—it would disappear.

So it is easy to see that even an argument trying to prove the non-existence of Consciousness could not exist without Consciousness. If you say that God does not exist, I ask you, Who is saying that God does not exist? It is God that says that God does not exist. So it is God Himself who is trying to prove that He does not exist. Why? Because that person who disproves the existence of Lord Śiva, by his very attempt to disprove His existence, proves His existence. This is because that person who is asking the question is Lord Śiva, who exists even before the question of His existence arises.

How can you understand the existence of Lord Śiva? You must comprehend it with your own understanding. Consider how His existence is shining everywhere, in agreement and in disagreement. If you agree that Lord Śiva exists, He is shining. If you do not agree that Lord Śiva exists, He is also shining in that disagreement. In both cases He is shining.

So, presenting an argument to prove His existence is also useless, because the person who is advancing the argument is that very being, already manifested there, who is being proven. Actually, the two classes of objects—internal and objective—and the three classes of bodies—gross, subtle, and subtlest—are dependent on that Consciousness. If Consciousness was not there, none of these objects or bodies would exist.[2]

2. The two classes of objects are external objects and internal objects. The external objective world consists of things, forms, colors, sounds, etc., which exist externally. The internal objective world is made up of pain, pleasures, grief, etc. Internal objects are those objects which are

And furthermore, a proof (*pramāṇa*) is only given for that which was not known previously and which is only known now. To give a proof for that which was already known before the existence of the proof does not make sense. Therefore, a proof of God, Lord Śiva, has no place here.

That complete I-Consciousness (*purnāhantā*) is filled with all sounds, all words, all sentences. Everything is existing there in that complete I-Consciousness. Hence, Paramaśiva is expanded in the cycle of thirty-six *tattvas,* elements. These thirty-six elements are as follows. First there are the pure elements *śiva, śakti, sadāśiva, iśvara* and *śuddhavidyā.* These are followed by the elements of limitation: ignorance (*māyā*), limited active energy (*kalā*), limited energy of knowledge (*vidyā*), attachment (*rāga*), limitation of time (*kāla*), and limitation of place (*niyati*).[3] After these are the *tattvas puruṣa*, limited soul, and *prakṛiti,* its nature. The *tattva buddhi* is intellect. *Ahaṁkāra* is ego. *Manas* is mind, *śrotra* is ear, *tvak* is skin, *cakṣuḥ* is eyes, *jihvā* is tongue, *ghrāṇa* is nose, *vāk* is sound, *pāṇi* is hand, *pāda* is feet, and *pāyu* is the organ of defecation. *Upastha* is the organ of urination. *Śabda* is sound, *sparśa* is touch, *rūpa* is form, *rasa* is taste, *gandha* is smell. *Ākāśa* is ether, *vāyu* is wind, *vahni* is fire, *salila* is water, and *bhūmi* is earth. These are thirty-six *tattvas,* and they are created in the nature of Lord Śiva.

Now I will explain these thirty-six *tattvas*. The first *tattva* is Śiva *tattva*, the element of Śiva. Śiva *tattva* is that *tattva* that is filled with *icchā*, will, *jñāna,* knowledge, and *kriyā*, action, each

---

not seen by anyone except that person who is experiencing them. Your internal objects are perceived by you alone. Your internal objects cannot be perceived by me. If you are filled with grief or happiness I cannot experience it nor can I see it. On the other hand, external objects are perceived by everyone.

There are also three classes of bodies: the gross body, the subtle body, and the subtlest body. The gross body is that body which is active in the waking state. The subtle body is that body which is active in the dreaming state. The subtlest body is that body which is active in the deep sleep state.

3. "Limitation of place" means being situated in a particular place, not in every place. It is a limitation of space.

of which is overflowing with complete ecstasy. His will is filled with ecstasy, His knowledge is filled with ecstasy, and His action is filled with ecstasy. This *tattva* is called *Paramaśiva.*

When the Supreme Lord (*Parameśvara*) wills to create this universe, which is existing in His nature, outside His nature in His own nature, the first start of the movement to create this universe is the element *śakti.* This is the first start of will (*icchā*). This will is the will of Lord Śiva. It is unencumbered will. For instance, you possess will and you want to shoot someone, but your will is fettered and you cannot shoot. On the other hand the will of Lord Śiva is free and independent. It is not limited or opposed by anyone. When He wills to create the universe the universe must come to be.

But this universe, which comes out from His nature, is already existing in His nature. When this universe first begins to sprout, it continues to be covered by the supreme I-Consciousness of Lord Śiva. In this sprouting of the universe, I-Consciousness is not ignored. At this stage of manifestation, I-Consciousness is predominant. This is the element of *sadāśiva.* The element *sadā-śiva* exists when the Lord perceives, "I am this universe." Not "I have created this universe" but rather "I am this universe." This is the state of *sadāśiva.*

When this universe, which is to be created, has sprouted in fullness, and yet is still wrapped with the I-Consciousness of Lord Śiva, this is the element *īśvara.*

When this universe is created and He sees that this created universe is not separate from Himself, and He feels the existence of His nature in the external universe, this is the element of *śuddhavidyā.*

You must note the difference between these three states: *sadāśiva, īśvara* and *śuddhavidyā. Sadāśiva* is that element which exists when universe is just about to sprout. It has not yet sprouted but it is going to sprout. This is the state of *sadāśiva.* When it has sprouted, this is the state of *īśvara.* When it has sprouted and it has bloomed in one's own nature, this is the state of *śuddhavidyā.*

The words *ahaṁ idam,* "I am this universe," express the experience in *sadāśiva.* The words *idam aham* signify "this universe is not separate from myself." This is the perception in the state of *īśvara*. The words *aham aham idam idam* mean "though this universe seems separate actually this universe is not separated from me." This is the experience in the state of *śuddhavidyā*.

So the universe is less predominant in *sadāśiva*, more predominant in *īśvara*, and most predominant in *śuddhavidyā*.

When you perceive that you know this universe, and when, because of this perception, you think that this universe is only an illusion—filled with pain and pleasure which must therefore be shunned—this kind of perception is called *māyā*. You must discard this perception, this *māyā*. *Māyā* is thinking that this universe is separate from your own nature. This is just illusion. It is ignorance.

When Lord Śiva, by His own free Energy (*svātantrya śakti*), envelopes His own nature with ignorance, He becomes a limited being. Then, in each and every way, He acts as if He were limited. In this limited state He feels, "Oh, this is my enemy, this is not my enemy; this is the truth, this is not the truth; this is good, this is bad." All these limitations and contradictions appear to Him. This is ignorance. In this state Lord Śiva is known as *purūṣa*, individual being.

When everything appears divine to you then you are Śiva. When everything appears as opposite, in contradiction, then you have become limited. At that point you are lost and there seems to be little hope for you. But even then there is hope. You can terminate and discard this limited state.

This individual is said to be deluded by his *māyā*, by his ignorance. Attached to his actions in his own way, he is a *saṁsārī*, a limited being (*jīva*), who wanders through this world in the cycle of repeated births and deaths. In these cycles there is no hope for him to rise in spirituality unless he yearns to rise. But when he yearns to rise, then he can rise.

In that state, as a limited being (*jīva*), he is also one with Lord Śiva. But because he is filled with ignorance he does not know that he is Lord Śiva. This is the problem of limited being. This kind of ignorance is not possible for Śiva. Although Śiva creates this universe and does everything, whether it is good or bad, he does not have ignorance. He does not think that He is separate from His own nature.

It is like the case of the accomplished magician: when you give this magician a handful of dust he will create a piece of candy for you. First he closes his fist around the dust, then he performs his magic. The result is that you will see his hand filled with candy. You must realize that only you see the candy, not the magician. He does not see candy. He will ask you, "Are these pieces of candy?" and you will say, "Yes, those are candies." But the magician does not see these pieces of candy, he only sees dust. The magician knows it is earth, but for you it is candy. You can even eat them, and they will be sweet. The magician cannot eat them because he knows that they are only earth. This is how this universe is created. For the magician it is earth. And for you who perceive this earth as candy, it is candy. You enjoy this candy, and yet it is nothing. It is only the existence of Lord Śiva. This universe is bondage for *jīva* and nothing for Lord Śiva.

In the same way, you see a beautiful wife or an ugly wife, a handsome man or an ugly man, a tasty fruit or a bad fruit. All these things you perceive in this way because of ignorance. But all of this is only his free independent Will, *svātantrya*, it is only the existence of Lord Śiva.

When, by the grace of Lord Śiva or the grace of his master, this limited being comes to the real understanding of his nature, then he knows that he is one with Paramaśiva. At that point there is no difference between him and Paramaśiva.

As the Supreme Lord (*parameśvara*), he possesses the five great energies. These five energies are the power of doing everything (*sarva-kartṛitvam*), the power of understanding everything (*sarva-jñatvam*), the power of complete fullness (*pūrṇatvam*), the power of eternality (*nityatvam*), and the power of being all-pervasive (*vyāpakatvam*). These are the energies that exist in Lord Śiva.

But, because of Śiva's magic, these energies assume different forms and conditions. The power of knowing everything (*sarva-jñatvam*) is transformed into the power of knowing something. The power of doing everything (*sarva-kartṛitvam*) is turned into the power of doing something. The power of complete fullness (*pūrṇatvam*) is transformed into the power of being incomplete, into the feeling of imperfection, of not being full. Due to the power of this limitation, the limited being may think, "I need this kind of fabric for my clothes otherwise I won't look right. If I don't loose weight and become physically fit everyone will see how ugly I am and no one will like me. I must own that automobile. If I own and drive that car everyone will respect me and see how successful I am." The power of being eternal (*nityatvam*) is transformed into power of ageing, of experiencing time. Due to this power the limited individual thinks, "I am thirty-five years old," when actually he is eternal. Time does not exist. It manifests only because of this limitation of the power of eternality. The power of being all-pervasive (*vyāpakatvam*) is transformed into the power of being limited in space, being in only one place and not everywhere.

When these powers, which are actually divine, take the form of limitation, they become the limitations *kalā, vidyā, rāga, kāla,* and *niyati. Kalā* is that which limits the Lord being able to do everything (*sarva-kartṛitvam*). *Vidyā* is that which limits His being all-knowing (*sarva-jñatvam*). *Rāga*, attachment, is that which limits His complete fullness (*pūrṇatvam*). Why? Because attachment arises when you are not full, when you feel that there is something lacking. *Kāla*, time, is that which limits His eternity (*nityatvam*). *Niyati* is that which limits His being all-pervasive (*vyāpakatvam*). It is a limitation of place. Actually you pervade everywhere but because of *niyati* you are found in only one place and nowhere else.

The limitation *kalā* leads the limited being to limited activity. The limitation *vidyā* leads him to limited knowledge. The limitation called *rāga* causes him to be attached to the five subtle elements (*tanmātras*),[4] sound (*śabda*), touch (*sparśa*), form (*rūpa*), taste (*rasa*), and smell (*gandha*).

The limitation of time, *kāla*, leads him to experience past, present, and future. He exists in the present. In the past he did not exist because he was not yet born. In the future he will not exist because he will have died. So it is the past, the present, and the future that hold him in their grasp.

---

4. *Tanmātras* are subtle elements, and potential states that exist as the ground of the five gross elements. They are the abode, the residence, of the sensations of the five senses.

The limitation *niyati* is limitation of action. "I have to do this, I will not do that." The limitation of action give rise to this kind of thinking and action.

These five elements of limitation are meant to cover and conceal His real nature. So they are called *kañcukas,* which means coverings.

These five *kañcukas,* the five elements of limitation (*kalā, vidyā, rāga, kāla, niyati*) along with *māyā,* comprise the six coverings (*ṣaṭ-kañcukas*) that cover His God Consciousness. Wearing these six coverings He becomes a completely limited being.

Following these six coverings in the succession of manifestation are the elements *prakṛiti* and *puruṣa.* These two elements are interdependent. *Prakṛiti,* often translated as "nature" or "primal matter," is the predominant cause (*mūla-kāraṇa*) of all other elements, beginning with the element intellect and ending with the final element earth. *Prakṛiti* is the undifferentiated potential that gives rise to the objective world, both internal and external. This is why in Sāṁkhya philosophy[5] the elements that are created by *prakṛiti* are called *vikṛiti. Vikṛiti* means that which has come into change. *Prakṛiti* is that which is changeless. *Prakṛiti* is the cause of *vikṛiti. Vikṛiti* is that which changes. *Prakṛiti* is unformed and assumes the form of that which changes. For example the element of the intellect changes, it is formed, in other words shaped, and this forming of *prakṛiti* is *vikṛiti.*

This *prakṛiti* is the state of undifferentiated equipose (*sāmyāvasthā*). It is that state where the three *guṇas—sattva, rajas,* and *tamas*—are not vividly perceived. These three *guṇas* exist in *prakṛiti,* but they are not perceived because, in *prakṛiti*, these elements are fully balanced and undifferentiated. These three *guṇas*, therefore, are not vividly manifested in the state of cause that is *prakṛiti.* That which responds to that *prakṛiti* and owns that *prakṛiti* is called *puruṣa. Puruṣa* is that bound and limited soul which is connected with subjectivity.

The element of intellect, *buddhi,* is that element which ascertains. First the movement of the mind appears as a thought and

5. The Sāṁkhya school of Indian philosophy is one of the six orthodox systems of classical Indian philosophy.

then that thought is reflected in the element of intellect (*buddhi*). When this thought is reflected in the intellect, this intellect determines whether we should act on this thought or not. This determination is accomplished by the intellect.

The next element after the intellect is *ahaṁkāra*, the element of ego. The element of ego is that element which causes you to think and understand that "this is mine and this is not mine." When this takes place you develop *abhimāna*, arrogance.

Following the ego is *manas*, the element of mind. Mind is that element which gives rise to endless varieties of purposeless and empty thoughts. You think, "This is a plug, this is a wall, this is a vase, this is a book." What do you have to do with all this useless thinking? You may think, "This is a tree." But you have nothing to do with the tree, yet the thought, "This is a tree," just rises in your mind. All thoughts such as, "This is cloth, this is this, this is that," are *saṁkalpa*[6] and are manufactured by *manas*, the element of mind.

These three—mind, ego, and intellect—are collectively called *antaḥkaraṇa*, which means "internal organ."

After the internal organs come the five perceptual organs. These five organs of perception[7]—ear, skin, eyes, tongue, and nose—control respectively the five *tanmātras*—sound, touch, form, taste, and smell.

Following the organs of perception the five organs of action are created. These organs of perception are the hand (*pāni*), the feet (*pāda*), the organ of excretion (*pāyū*), the organ of generation (*upastha*), and the tongue (*vāk*). *Vāk* produces two organs, one organ of perception and one organ of action. When perception is produced by the tongue it is taste. When action is produced by the tongue it is speech. In this work this is expressed by the word *vacana*. *Ādāna* is holding, which is accomplished by the hands. *Viharaṇa*, moving here and there, is accomplished by the feet. *Visarga*, excretion, though it is two actions, is accomplished by

6. *Saṁkalpa* is intentional thought, conscious, directed thought.

7. In order, the five organs of perception are *śrotra, tvak, cakṣuḥ, jihvā,* and *ghrāṇa*. The five *tanmātrās* are *śabda, sparśa, rūpa, rasa,* and *gandha.*

one organ. When you urinate and when you pass stools, both acts are excretion and both are accomplished by only one organ. The organ of sex gives rise to the ecstasy (*ānanda*) of sex. It is the organ of ecstasy.

The elements coming after the five organs of action are the five *tanmātras*. The *tanmātras* are the abode, or residence, of the sensations of the five senses. For example, after I produce the sound *oṁ,* where does this sound go? It has taken residence in *śabda-tanmātra,* it remains in *śabda-tanmātra,* and it can be created again from that *tanmātra*. That sound can be withdrawn again, and it can be produced and heard again. Whatever we say is stored in *śabda-tanmātra*. *Śabda-tanmātra* is the residence of the impression of sound. This is also the case for the other four *tanmātras*. *Sparśa-tanmātra* is the abode of touch, the sensation of touch. *Rasa-tanmātra* is the abode of the impression of taste. *Rūpa-tanmātra* is the abode of the impression of form, and *gandha-tanmātra* is the residence of the impression of smell.

After the five *tanmātras* come the five gross elements.[8] These elements are ether, wind, fire, water, and earth. The element ether gives you space to walk and to move. If there were no ether, you could not move your hand or your arm. So ether gives you room. The element wind gives you life. The element of fire gives you heat and burning sensation. The element of water gives you wetness and cooling life. It gives you a life-full cold sensation, and it moisturizes you when you are dry. The element of earth will hold you. If there were no earth, nothing would be held.

The Essence of the Thirty-Six Elements

At this point the author Kṣemarāja has completed his explanation of the thirty-six elements. Now he begins his clarification of the essence of these thirty-six elements.

To begin with, you must understand that in the field of *mantras*, in the field of sacred words, the *mantra* that digests these thirty-six elements in its body is *sauḥ*. It is the supreme

---

8. In order, the five gross elements are *ākāsa, vāyu, agni, jala,* and *pṛithvī.*

mantra. It is not a creative *mantra*; it is a destructive *mantra*. Why? Because it winds up the complete cycle of the thirty-six elements. This *mantra* shows you the trick of how to wind up, how to discard, these thirty-six elements and, in the end, rest in the element of Śiva. So it is not expansion, it is winding up. And this winding up is not actually destruction, it is contraction, just as a giant tree is contracted in a seed.

In this regard Kṣemarāja gives the example of the seed of the *nyagrodha* tree. The *nyagrodha* tree is a giant and majestic fig tree with a trunk ten times bigger than that of a *chinar* tree.[9] But this *nyagrodha* tree, which is so very huge, produces very tiny seeds. And yet within these seeds exist the strength and the power to produce that giant tree.

In this way the entire universe consisting of thirty-six elements[10] resides in the *mantra sauḥ*. This *mantra* is called the heart *mantra* because it is the essence of all *mantras*. How is this so? In the same way that a clay bowl or a clay plate are only produced by changing earthen clay, the essence of this bowl or plate continues to be clay. Or, just as ice and vapor, which are produced by watery substances, are actually water.

So, in the realm of the supreme *mantra sauḥ*, if you go into the depth of the thirty-one elements from *pṛithivī* (earth) to *māyā,* you will find that existence (*sat*) is the reality of these elements. All these elements are all existing externally.

Now Kṣhemarāja tells us that the word *sat* has a deeper meaning than is usually understood. *Sat* consists of two parts,

---

9. The *chinar* tree is a magnificent and immense deciduous tree of the maple family native to the valley of Kashmir.

10. In this realm of the supreme *mantra sauḥ,* the thirty-six *tattvas* are classified in three parts. The first part of the *mantra sauḥ* is *"sat."* The second part of the *mantra sauḥ* is *au*. *Au* contains the fourteen Sanskrit vowels *a ā i ī u ū ṛi ṛī li lī e ai o* and *au*. And the third part of the *mantra sauḥ* is *visarga,* the Sanskrit letter *ḥ*. These three *s* (*at*) + *au* + *ḥ* constitute the supreme (*parā*) *mantra sauḥ,* and they respectively digest all of the thirty-six elements. Thirty-one elements, from *pṛithvī* to *māyā*, are digested by *sat*. Three elements, *śuddhavidhyā, īśvara,* and *sadāśiva* are digested by *au*. And two elements, *śiva* and *śakti,* are digested by *visarga ḥ*.

sa and the suffix *at*. In this case the suffix *at* is only present to help with pronounciation. If we discard the suffix we are left with only *sa*. *Sa* comes from the Sanskrit verbal root *as* (to be). *As*, the verbal root, is designated in grammar as *bhuvi*, that is, meant for existence (*bhuvi*). That which is existing is called *asti*, "It is."

So, by leaving the suffix *at* aside, only *sa* remains. You have to discern that the thirty-one elements reside in the first word *sa*. These thirty-one elements are the embodiment of *nara*, the individual.

After this, you must ascertain that residing in the second part of the *mantra sauḥ* is the letter *au*, which is superior to *sa*, and which contains the elements *śuddhavidyā, īśvara,* and *sadāśiva.* These three elements are the essence of knowledge (*jñāna*) and action (*kriyā*). They are the embodiment of *śakti.*

The letter *au* is *abhyupagama*, acceptance, it is the acceptance of the oneness of God Consciousness. This oneness of God Consciousness is not accepted in the thirty-one elements. The thirty-one elements are scattered. So they have not accepted the unbroken reality of God Consciousness. When you accept the oneness of God Consciousness, you digest it in your nature. Acceptance is the key. You have to recognize it, you have to digest it in your own nature. You will digest it only in *śuddhavidyā, īśvara,* and *sadśāśiva*. This is the meaning of *abhyupagama*, acceptance.

Greater than the letter *au*, and residing in the third part of the *mantra sauḥ*, is the letter *ḥ,* a creative energy which is twofold. This twofold, creative energy is comprised of a higher creative energy and a lower creative energy. The higher creative energy is of *śiva* and the lower creative energy is of *śakti.* This two-part creative energy, above and below, are the two points of the Sanskrit *visargaḥ.*[11]

The first part of the *mantra sauḥ, sa,* is in the cycle of *nara;* the second part of the *mantra sauḥ, au*, is in the cycle of *śakti;* and the third part of the *mantra sauḥ, ḥ,* combining both of the cre-

11. In Devanāgari, the script of the Sanskrit language, the letter *visargaḥ* is written as two points, thus " : ".

ative energies, is in the cycle of *śiva*. So, the Trika system of Kashmir Śaivism is the combination of *nara, śakti,* and *śiva.*

In this way this seed *mantra*, *sauḥ,* is the supreme *mantra*. It is above all other *mantras* including the blessed *mantras ahaṁ, oṁ,* and *so'ham*. This supreme *mantra*, which is both universal (*viśvamaya*) and transcendent (*viśvottīrṇa*) is the essence of Trika. Lord Śiva, the supreme reality, is therefore the state of flowing out and resting.

Thus, whoever perceives *sauḥ,* the essence of all *mantras*, in the reality of *samādhi*,[12] gains entry in that *sa*. He is, in the real sense, initiated. It does not matter if he lives and breathes like an ordinary being, if he gets hungry and attends to his bodily functions, he is actually divine, and at the time of leaving his physical form he becomes one with Śiva.

---

12. *Sauḥ* is perceived in *samādhi* only in the state of *jagad-ānanda*.

FOUR

Talks on Discipline

1. The Five *Niyamas*

When we study the Śaiva Scriptures we must always remember that these scriptures were narrated by Lord Śiva Himself in the form of Svacchandanātha. In this form Lord Śiva narrated these scriptures with His five mouths, symbolizing His five great energies. These are the energy of consciousness (*cit-śakti*), the energy of bliss (*ānanda-śakti*), the energy of will (*icchā-śakti*), the energy of knowledge (*jñāna-śakti*), and the energy of action (*kriyā-śakti*). These five mouths are called the five forms of Svacchandanātha and are individually referred to as Īśāna, Tatpurūṣa, Sadyojāta, Vāmadeva, and Aghora.

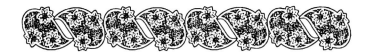

The scriptures, called Tantras in our Śaivism, were created by these five great mouths. They are classified into three divisions depending on whether the knowledge they contain is monistic (*abheda*), monistic cum dualistic (*bhedābheda*), or dualistic (*bheda*). The monistic (*abheda*) Tantras are known as the Bhairava Tantras, the monistic cum dualistic (*bhedābheda*) Tantras are known as the Rudra Tantras, and the dualistic (*bheda*) Tantras are known as the Śiva Tantras. There are sixty-four Bhairava Tantras, eighteen Rudra Tantras, and ten Śiva Tantras, making a total of ninety-two Tantras. Remember that all these Tantras, whether *abheda, bhedābheda,* or *bheda*, are the creation of Lord Śiva Himself in the form of Svacchandanātha.

Svacchandanātha, while creating these Tantras through His five mouths, possessed eighteen arms. These eighteen arms are symbols of the eighteen elements or *tattvas*. These *tattvas* are offshoots of His five great *śaktis* and are created in the following manner. *Cit-śakti* gives rise to one element, *manas-tattva*, the element of mind. *Ānanda-śakti* gives rise to two elements, *buddhi* and *ahaṁkāra,* the elements of intellect and ego. *Icchā-śakti* gives rise to five elements, which are the five vital airs (*vāyu*) of the body. These are *prāṇa, apāna, samāna, udāna,* and *vyāna. Jñāna-śakti* also gives rise to five elements, known as the *jñānendriyas;* these are the five elements of knowledge, which are smell (*ghrāṇa*), taste (*jihvā*), touch (*tvak*), sight (*cakṣuḥ*), and hearing (*śrotra*). *Kriyā-śakti* gives rise to the five elements of action, the five *karmendriyas*. These include the organ of generation (*upastha*), the organ of excretion (*pāyu*), the organ of mobility (*pāda*), the organ of holding (*pāṇi*), and the organ of speech (*vāk*). These eighteen arms of Lord Śiva, in the form of Svacchandanātha, are created by Lord Śiva for the protection of the individual, but in order to receive this protection the individual must adhere to divine discipline.

This divine discipline is comprised of the five *niyamas* and the five *yamas*. You can only gain the protection of the Lord by strictly following the code of conduct set forth in these *niyamas* and *yamas*. This is not something I made up but a statement of fact. I will now explain the five *niyamas*. These are *śauca, santoṣa, tapasya, svādhyāya,* and *īśvara-praṇidhāna*.

Śauca

Śauca means clean or cleanliness. It is the essence of purity: purity of the body, mind, and speech. To keep the body clean is essential for God Consciousness. It does not matter if your clothes are not luxurious and expensive, but the garments you wear must be spotlessly clean. The mind must also be cleaned and purified of all wretched and irreverent thoughts. If a wrong thought should intrude into your mind you must try to brush it away by thinking of righteous persons and their teachings, or about the great sages and saints who have left such a treasure of teachings. The mind should not be disturbed by a myriad of thoughts (*vikalpa*); it should be pure, clean, and simple.

By purity of speech I mean that the words you use should not excite anger or wrath in others. Speech should be used to express only that which is true, which is best, which is correct—only that which is full of absolute purity. Speech should not be used to hurl abuses at others or to give expression to language which is disgusting or base. Your speech should be used to express words of sweetness and piety, to express that which uplifts and never harms another.

These three—purity of body, mind, and speech—are so completely interlinked that even if one aspect of these three is followed with fervor and enthusiasm it will inevitably help in developing the other two. Together these will help push you toward the ultimate result—concentration and God Consciousness. Patañjali has said:

> *The fruit that accrues from maintaining cleanliness* (śauca) *of body, mind, and action is that you will begin to hate your body and shun contact with other bodies.*[1]
>
> Yoga Sūtra 2:40

If one is determined to maintain an absolutely clean body then he will begin to hate his body. Why? When one has cleaned his skin thoroughly with soap and water, he will think that he is quite clean and will, therefore, enter into his meditation room. Once inside, however, he begins coughing up phlegm. He realizes then, at that moment, that though he is clean outside he is dirty inside. He begins to want to be rid of his body, and this develops into the desire to disassociate himself from his family and relatives. He prefers seclusion above all else. This is the attainment gained by cleanliness.

---

1. śaucātsvaṅgajugupsā parairasaṁsargaḥ //

Santoṣa

Santoṣa means contentment, real satisfaction. It is the opposite of greed, the desire and craving for more and more. You should be satisfied with whatever you have. You must take whatever little you possess as a gift from the Lord. You must accept that gift with pleasure. The Lord knows what to give, how much should be given, and how to give it. He is the great distributor of all that we possess. Therefore, you should not think that you have too few possessions but rather you should think that what you do possess is sufficient for your needs, because the Lord knows what is best for you. You will receive only as much as you deserve according to the justice of the Lord, no more and no less. It is human weakness to think, "My life is ruined for I have not been promoted in my job," or, "I am so sad that I didn't get the clothes that I wanted." Think that whatever you have is the gift of Lord Śiva and that whatever He has thought best for you He has given to you. If you think in this way you will be satisfied; you will cease craving for more and more and will enter into the realm of peace and tranquility. Everything in this universe belongs to Lord Śiva—all wealth, all luxury, everything. He distributes in His own right way and gives to you what is best for you. So why concern yourself with unnecessary craving?

> *The fruit that accrues from maintaining complete contentment* (santoṣa) *is that you attain complete peace in this lifetime.*[2]
>
> Yoga Sūtra 2:42

A person can be happy and content only if he wills it. Even though it may seem difficult a man can even be content and sleep peacefully on a rock.

Tapasya

Tapasya means self-control and tolerance, not yielding to temptation as a glutton does to his desire for more food. It is my advice

2. santoṣādanuttamasukhalābhaḥ //

that you should not overeat by filling yourself with excess food. You should leave your stomach slightly empty, eat slightly less. This will keep your body in form and your mind agile and alert. Otherwise you will become baggy just like a sack of food. You will waste away your time yawning and feeling sleepy. You cannot maintain the proper strength of concentration or meditation when your body is in this state.

Gandhiji has said, "This world crushes the dust under its feet, but the seeker of truth should be humbler than the dust." He should be so humble that even the dust should crush him, such should be his self-control. This self-control is real *tapasya* and is the essence of patience and tolerance. Without it you cannot meditate. You will only burp like a cow. By self-control, you must dissolve the dust of your mind. About this self-control Patañjali has said:

> *The fruit acquired through practicing self-control and tolerance* (tapas) *is that all impurity in your body and organs will vanish and you will become filled with power.*[3]
>
> Yoga Sūtra 2:43

Svādhyāya

Svādhyāya, the fourth *niyama*, means self-knowing. You should not waste your energies by being talkative. You should shun frivolous talk, such as talking about social concerns, dowry matters, or the like. Wasting energy on useless and futile things is a sin. You should devote your time to studying and reflecting upon scriptures of Kashmir Śaivism and the *Bhagavad Gītā*. You should try to know yourself by understanding yourself.

> *The fruit that accrues from continuously striving for self-knowledge by constant study of the scriptures is*

3. kāyendriyasiddhiraśuddhikṣayāttapasaḥ //

> *that the Lord whom you seek* (iṣṭadeva) *will shine before you.*[4]
>
> Yoga Sūtra 2:44

Whether your Lord is Śiva, Rāma, or Kṛiṣna, He will reveal Himself to you, either in the dreaming state or in wakefulness.

> *I bow to those devotees who in their dreams experience Lord Śiva, the bestower of all bliss and peace, with the crescent moon shining on His forehead.*[5]
>
> Stavacintāmaṇi 13

Īśvara-praṇidhāna

Īśvara-praṇidhāna is the final and supreme *niyama*. It means love and devotion to God. The love of Lord Śiva creates devotion. If you love Lord Śiva and are devoted to Him, it is not possible for Him to neglect you. He will reveal Himself to you and purify you with his glorious eighteen arms. He will help you enter into the realm of God Consciousness.

> *Through devotion to Lord Śiva, mystical rapture* (samādhi) *is effortlessly attained.*[6]
>
> Yoga Sūtra 2:45

To enable yourself to be protected by the eighteen arms of Lord Śiva, you must endeavor to protect yourself through the above *niyamas,* as I have outlined. Do not worry about material things or about your family or relatives. You must concentrate one-pointedly on God. When you do so, God will most certainly reveal Himself to you.

---

4. svādhyāyādiṣṭadevatāsaṁprayogaḥ //
5. namastebhyo'pi ye
   somakalākalitaśekharaṁ /
   nāthaṁ svapne'pi paśyanti
   paramānandadāyinam //
6. samādhisiddhirīśvarapraṇidhānāt //

2. The Five Moral Prescriptions

> *It is not the case that the Lord of death will snatch only those who have enjoyed a long span of life. He can touch anyone, whether he be an embryo, a child, an adolescent, or an adult. This is the way of the world.*[7]
>
> Kulārṇava Tantra 9

Mahākāla, the wheel of destruction, visits everyone, everywhere. It has never been stopped by anyone. The meaning of this verse is that every living entity, an embryo in the womb, an infant, a child, a young adult, or an aged person, are all easily reached by the hand of Death. The hand of Death can reach anyone, anywhere. This is the way of the world, so why worry about anything? Be happy. A person is just like a clod of earth, which when struck by rain mixes with the ground and loses its independent personality. It collapses and is dissolved into nothingness. Nothing is permanent, so why be greedy? Why become the victim of temptation, hoard possessions, and become filled with lies?

In the last talk I told you about the five *niyamas*. Now I want to tell you about the five *yamas*, the five moral prescriptions: *ahiṁsā, satya, asteya, brahmacarya* and *aparigraha*.

Ahiṁsā

Ahiṁsā means non-violence. Non-violence is of two kinds, gross and subtle. Subtle non-violence is that non-violence where the effects of one's actions or words are taken into account. For example, it is a form of violence if your words or actions harm another's psyche or cause anger or hatred in them. This kind of violence is subtle in nature. You should be humble and soft spoken. You should discipline yourself and keep from inflicting subtle pain,

---

7. bālāṁśca yauvanasthāṁśca
vṛiddhān garbhagatānapi /
sarvānāviśate mṛityu-
revaṁbhūtaṁ jagadidam //

which is harmful. Maintaining this subtle non-violence does not permit you to deal with others in a loud and shrill manner.

This subtle non-violence must be followed through a strict discipline of the body, mind, and soul. One who maintains this discipline of subtle non-violence in body, mind, and soul, and is established in this discipline, influences even natural enemies by his presence. Such is his vibrating power. For example, if a cat and a mouse are in the presence of such a person, though they are bitter enemies, and the tendency is for the cat to attack the mouse and for the mouse to attempt to escape, they both remain placid and harmless. The cat does not attack the mouse and the mouse does not run. This is the all-pervasive power of non-violence, which permeates these creatures in the presence of a person or spiritual aspirant who is established in the discipline of non-violence.

> *No power on earth can make two mutual enemies enter into combat in the presence of him who, being established in subtle non-violence, does not harm anyone.*[8]
>
> Yoga Sūtra 2:35

Gross non-violence is the shunning of that which is the worst of all violence, the killing of a living being, the taking of its life for the pleasure of eating it. There is no greater sin than this. To be really established in non-violence, you must give up meat-eating. You must shun it completely. You must be a complete vegetarian. It is a fact that the fruit of meditation can only be possessed by a pure vegetarian.

All those involved, in any way, with the acts of killing, preparing, and eating meat are equally guilty and equally depraved and criminal. Every aspect of this act is wrong. Even those who witness the act of killing or witness the act of eating meat are criminals. I cannot impress upon you strongly enough how sinful and wrong is the act of eating meat. The butcher, the cook, the final consumer, even the witness of any of these acts, are all sinners.

---

8 ahiṁsāpratiṣṭhāyāṁ tatsannidhau vairatyāgaḥ //

Plate 14. Swami Lakshmanjoo in 1991.

You may think that only the butcher who has actually slaughtered the animal is a sinner. You are wrong. Any person involved in any way is equally a sinner and a criminal in this most terrible, violent act of killing. Take one small piece of meat and you are just like the butcher himself. You both belong to the same class. About this there is no doubt. Even if you may be a vegetarian, and yet you do not oppose this act of extreme violence, you are a sinner judged to have committed the same crime.

> *Even if you are not a thief and yet you associate with thieves you are also considered to be a thief.*[9]
>
> Tantrāloka

A person who, even though he is a vegetarian, is sociable with butchers, maintaining friendly contacts with them, is also a sinner and receives punishment. So it is your duty not only to maintain a strict vegetarian life-style but also to loudly oppose the killing of animals and the eating of meat. You must communicate my message and this truth to everyone who is near and dear to you, to all your relatives, mothers and fathers, sons and daughters.

Yājñavalkya tells us in his *Yājñavalkyasmṛiti* that there are three ghastly crimes committed in the slaughtering of animals for the enjoyment of eating their flesh. These crimes are *prāṇāharaṇa, pīḍā,* and *vīryākṣepa. Prāṇāharaṇa* is the crime of taking life away from an animal, removing its life though it is innocent, though it has done nothing to deserve having its life taken away. *Pīḍā* is the crime of inflicting great pain on an animal while killing it. *Vīryākṣepa* is the crime of taking away its strength.

The scriptures have also indicated the punishment to be given to those guilty of committing these three crimes. Those who are guilty of committing the crime of *prāṇāharaṇa,* the crime of taking away life, will be punished for twenty rebirths by having to experience in each rebirth premature death, dying in infancy or in early or middle life. These deaths are not peaceful. They are filled with pain and suffering.

---

9. yathāhyatanmayo'pyeti
pātitāṁ taiḥ samāgamāt

Plate 15. Swami Lakshmanjoo with Shanna Hughes in 1991.

Plate 16. Swami Lakshmanjoo with Shanna Hughes in 1973.

The punishment for those guilty of the crime of *pīḍā,* inflicting physical pain and agony, is that for twenty lifetimes they themselves will undergo pain and torture. Their lives will be filled with disharmony and struggle. They will not experience peace of mind but will experience the torture of family feuds and the like. They will be unhappy and helpless, filled with tension and anxiety, experiencing life with uneasiness and uncertainty. For those guilty of the crime of *vīryākṣepa,* the taking of an animal's strength through slaughtering it, the punishment is that they will experience, for twenty lifetimes, lives which are devoid of strength or health. They will become void and wasted like the living dead. These are the punishments exacted for the three heinous crimes that accrue to one who eats meat. This is why we call meat *maṁsa,* as it is said, *"māṁ sa atti,"* which means "He will eat me."

Sages and saints of old teach us that the one whose flesh you eat in this world will eat you in the next world.[10]

Manusmṛiti 5:15

This means that if you eat the flesh of an animal, that animal will not release you. He will follow you even to other worlds (*para-loka*); he will chase you continuously, without break, not only for one lifetime, but for twenty lifetimes. In these twenty lifetimes you, who have eaten the flesh of this animal, will experience the punishments I have indicated. Manu in his *Manusmṛiti* expresses an even stronger viewpoint. He says:

Count the hairs of the animal you have killed and eaten, and for that many lifetimes you will be killed by that animal.[11]

Manusmṛiti 5:38

And he says further,

He who avoids meat eating for his whole life receives the same meritorious fruit after death as he who adopts the aśvamedha *sacrifice every year for one hundred years.*[12]

Manusmṛiti 5:53

---

10. māṁsabhakṣayitāmutra
yasya māṁsaṁihādmyaham /
etanmāṁsasya māṁsatvaṁ
pravadanti manīṣiṇaḥ //
11. yāvanti paśulomāni
tāvatkṛitvo ha māraṇam /
vṛithā paśughnaḥ prāpnoti
pretya janmani janmani //
12. varṣe varṣe'śvamedhena
yo yajeta śataṁ samāḥ /
māṁsāni ca na khādedyaḥ
tayoḥ puṇyaphalaṁ samam //

Can you understand? A person performs an *aśvamedha* sacrifice every year for his whole life. How virtuous and sinless he must be! Yet that person who abstains from eating meat, is higher, more sinless, more virtuous than he who performs the yearly *aśvamedha* sacrifice.[13]

It is also said elsewhere in our Śaivism:

> *You should not kill animals at the time of marriage celebration, or for your own self-satisfaction, or in rituals, or in hosting your dear loved ones.*[14]
>
> Jayaratha's commentary on Tantrāloka 14

You should not serve meat on marriage occasions, nor should you fool yourself into thinking that you must take meat for reasons of health. This is no reason. Why should you kill an innocent being because of your disbelief and fear of death. It is better that you die than try to preserve your own life by taking the life of an innocent being. Some of you may say, "But I must serve meat to my guests, such as my son-in-law, or they will be insulted. They will think that I have been miserly, refusing to spend properly for their entertainment and enjoyment." I tell you this, if you really love your son-in-law or your guests, entertain them with delicious vegetarian dishes, with a variety of vegetables, cheese and yogurt. Do not entertain them with meat dishes. Giving them meat dishes does not show that you love them but rather it shows that you hate them, for you are encouraging those evil acts that will send them to hell for twenty lifetimes.

You may also say, "We have a problem and our priest, who is a well-read *paṇḍit* (scholar), has recommended that we sacrifice a

---

13. The *aśvamedha* ("horse sacrifice") was an ancient Vedic sacrifice performed to assure the favor of the gods. In early times it was considered a very auspicious and powerful ritual. Horses were actually sacrificed in this ritual, yet, because these sacrifices were offered to the gods, they were believed to be sinless and pure.

14. na vivāhe paśuṁ hanyān-
na cātmārthe kadācan /
yāgakāle ca na hanyāt
neṣṭabandhusamāgame //

sheep, and that this sacrifice will absolve us from any danger or fear." I say that this is all nonsense, irrelevant and meaningless. My own father went to the shrine at Khrew[15] and worshipped there along with others by offering the lungs of sheep. At that time, I thought how deluded they were to believe that they would reach heaven after creating so much pain and suffering, by spilling the blood of an innocent and speechless lamb. Hence do not eat meat. This is real nonviolence (*ahiṁsā*).

Satya

Satya means truth, both objective and internal. By objective truth I do not mean truth that will create destruction or animosity. Truth should spread peace and tranquility. So the truth should be spoken according to the time and circumstances. And yet, you should also not lie, as it is a weakness and a sin. You should act to avoid uttering those truths that will only create problems.

Internal truth is of a different kind. It is truthful meditation. For example, thieves rob your mind while you are meditating. They deprive you of your valuables, your awareness. Hence you should not meditate keeping your eyes closed. What do I mean by keeping your eyes closed? I mean losing consciousness, losing attentive awareness. You should meditate with full consciousness, otherwise you will be robbed by the thieves of the mind. They will deprive you of your concentration and break your awareness by creating a veil of temptations and random thoughts. These are the internal robbers against whom you must always be vigilant. Closing your eyes and not knowing what is happening, not knowing how thieves are robbing your self-awareness, is untrue internal meditation.

> *If, after withdrawing your organs of action and your organs of cognition, you internally stimulate yourself*

---

15. Khrew is a village located about fifteen kilometers southeast of Srinagar, Kashmir. Situated on top of a rocky summit on the outskirts of Khrew is a shrine dedicated to the worship of Jvālā Devī. To this day this worship is accomplished primarily through the sacrifice of sheep.

Plate 17. Swami Lakshmanjoo with Denise Hughes in 1991.

> *with thoughts of sensual pleasures, then you are on the wrong path. Your activities are meaningless and have no value.*[16]
>
> Bhagavad Gītā 3:6

Whosoever does not utter falsehood even by chance or error has great power in his utterance. Whatever he says is fulfilled, fulfilled by his nature of truth. Whatever he desires and gives expression to is fulfilled and is achieved by him. He may say to a person, "May God bless you," and God blesses that person. Thus, his truthfulness always bears fruit.

Asteya

Asteya means not being dishonest. By dishonesty I do not simply mean physical dishonesty or thievery, as when your objective pos-

---

16. karmendriyāṇi saṁyamya ya āste manasā smaran /
indriyārthān vimūḍhātmā mūḍhācāraḥ sa ucyate //

sessions are stolen by burglars during the night. There is also mental theft. Greed due to temptation is theft, as is jealousy and envy. They involve the contemplation of gaining material benefit at the cost of others, or the desire to seize status or respect from another. Trying to attain what you do not deserve, or trying to accomplish for yourself an objective without regard for others, or depriving others of what is rightfully theirs by blackmail, or the maneuvering of influence, are all forms of theft. This mental theft is just as wrong as physical theft. Both should be avoided.

You will have everything in abundance if you do not crave another's possessions. As Patañjali teaches:

> *The fruit of being established in honesty is that all luxury will automatically be at your disposal.*[17]
>
> Yoga Sūtra 2:37

As we are taught in the *Bhagavad Gītā*:

> *Upon those who adore me with alertness, never forgetting me, I easily bestow that intellectual clarity by which they achieve me, and by which they also can cause others to achieve me.*[18]
>
> Bhagavad Gītā 10:10

Here Lord Kṛiṣṇa is telling us that those who are established in this form of honesty will achieve whatever they need or want. He teaches us, therefore, that the Lord protects those who are truly honest by providing for them completely.

> *This whole universe, along with its substances, is directed and pervaded by Lord Śiva. Whatever exists is His property, and therefore whatsoever out of that property He, according to His choice, bestows upon you,*

---

17. asteya pratiṣṭhāyāṁ sarvaratnopasthānam //
18. teṣāṁ satatayuktānāṁ bhajatāṁ prītipūrvakam /
dadāmi buddhiyogaṁ taṁ yena māṁ prāpayanti te //

> *enjoy it. Do not covet another's property. For, after all, whatever exists is not the property of anyone except Lord Śiva.*[19]
>
> Īśa Upaniṣad 1

All that exists in this universe, whether it be material property, or your family or friends, is owned and possessed by Lord Śiva. He has allowed you to possess temporarily whatever you have. Therefore make the best use of whatever He has loaned to you. Do not be jealous. Be satisfied and content. He has distributed everything according to His own will. This is the divine law of distribution. Bow to His order, His Law of Distribution, and establish yourself in honesty.

Brahmacarya

Brahmacarya means the maintenance of mental and physical character. It means not yielding to sensual temptation, not allowing the mode of sensual desire to capture your mind. For example, a man should not desire to have intercourse with any woman other than his own wife, nor should a woman look at any man other than her husband. To do so takes them away from being established in the state of *brahmacarya*. But what is the point of this state of *brahmacarya*? Why is it important to cultivate this aspect of your character? Through cultivating *brahmacarya* you attain what is known as the storage of power (*vīrya-lābha*). Patañjali has said:

> *The fruit of being established in* brahmacarya *in mind, action, and words is that your word becomes true.*[20]
>
> Yoga Sūtra 2:38

This power, this vital energy (*vīrya*) gives you strength. Not strength to be used for physical or social activities, but strength for spiritual activities.

---

19. īśāvāsyam idaṁ sarvaṁ yat kiñcij jagatyāṁ jagat /
tena tyaktena bhuñjīthā mā gṛidhaḥ kasyasvid dhanam //
20. brahmacaryapratiṣṭhāyāṁ vīrayalābhaḥ //

Plate 18. Swami Lakshmanjoo with John Hughes in 1991.

> *If your conduct of remembering God is protected for the sake of duty, and your duty is protected for the sake of knowing Lord Śiva, and your knowledge is protected for the sake of contemplation, then without doubt you will quickly gain liberation.*[21]
>
> Kulārṇava Tantra

God will visit you often if the *vīrya* you have preserved is utilized for God Consciousness. That *vīrya* that you possess must be utilized for knowledge (*jñāna*). This is not knowledge for use in debates or for subduing others through the show of your power of understanding. This knowledge is for the pursuit of God Consciousness, which when possessing this power, is easily attained and liberation quickly gained. It is said that if a real *brahmacārī* is instructed in meditation by his master, meditation will bear fruit for him easily and quickly. On the other hand if a person

21. tadgopitaṁ syād dharmārthaṁ
dharmaṁ jñānārthameva ca /
jñānaṁ tu dhyānayogārthaṁ
so'cirātpravimucyate //

with no character, who is not *brahmacarya,* attempts to practice meditation, he will either doze, and thereby fall asleep, or he will be wavering and his mind will always be unsettled. The *brahmacārī* has great power of concentration. He can attain in one hour what the fellow without character cannot achieve in twenty years. The *brahmacārī* can easily attain God Consciousness.

Therefore *brahmacarya* is a precious jewel. It must be protected and guarded. Physical and sensual temptation can harm and kill the *brahmacarya* in a person. Through concentration he gains entry into the state of oneness *(tanmaya)*, which is essential for gaining entry into the divine .

There is a story in the *Rāmāyaṇa* that illustrates the character of *brahmacarya.* When Rāvaṇa kidnapped Sītā from her *ashram* in the jungle, Rāma and Lakṣmaṇa searched the whole jungle. Near by—on the other side of a mountain called Riṣi Mukha—Sugrīva, Hanumān, and a group of monkeys were sitting on the ground when Rāvaṇa, who was carrying Sītā through the sky in his chariot, happened to fly overhead. Sītā at that moment cast her ornaments and jewelry to the ground with the thought that Rāma, wandering in the forest, might find these jewels and ornaments, and thereby come to know the route by which she was abducted.

Some of these ornaments fell where Sugrīva and Hanumān were sitting. They ran and found the fallen ornaments and showed them to Rāma and Lakṣmaṇa when they came to that part of the forest. Rāma immediately recognized the ornaments as Sītā's. To confirm his identification he asked Lakṣmaṇa if he recognized the ornaments. Lakṣmaṇa replied,

> *I cannot recognize the ornaments which she wore in her ears or on her wrist. I can only recognize the ornaments she wore on her feet and nothing else. I have never seen her face.*[22]
>
> Vālmīki Rāmāyaṇa

Such should be the character (*brahmacarya*) of a person.

---

22. nāhaṁ jānāmi keyure
nāhaṁ jāṇāmi kuṇḍale /
nūpure tvabhijānāmi
nityaṁ tatpādavandanāt //

Aparigraha

Aparigraha means the absence of the habit and disease of hoarding. We all hoard too much. The more things you hoard the more you will be worried and preoccupied for their preservation and care. For example, a shovel of ours is broken and we store the broken piece in our storehouse; or we break the frame of our glasses and store away the broken piece. We are such hoarders that we cannot leave our home. We should discard all these useless items.

> *The fruit which accrues when you are established in the state marked by the absence of hoarding* (aparigraha) *is that you become able to know your past, present, and future.*[23]
>
> Yoga Sūtra 2:39

The person who does not hoard has his vision expanded to encompass three lifetimes. With clarity he can review the past, look into the present, and foresee the future. He becomes clairvoyant. This is the power that comes to one who does not hoard.

I have clearly and succinctly set out the requirements necessary for establishing yourself in the discipline and state of the *yamas* and *niyamas*. If you carefully follow what I have said, there is no question that Lord Śiva in the form of Svacchandanātha will protect you with His wonderful eighteen arms and, through His shining Grace, reveal Himself to you.

---

23. aparigrahasthaire janmakathantāsambodhaḥ //

FIVE

The Secret Knowledge of Kuṇḍalinī

SEVERAL YEARS AGO I GAVE A TALK ON *kuṇḍalinī*[1] to the *paṇḍits* and scholars attending a Tantric conference in Varanasi. I started my talk by saying, "Today I will, according to my intellect, according to what I have experienced, and according to the grace of my masters, put before you who are soaked in the secrets of Śaivism, something of the knowledge of *kuṇḍalinī*. Please hear it attentively, with awareness." I then began the body of my address with this auspicious verse:

> *Kaulikī Kuṇḍalinī is revealed in the Kula system. This Kaulikī Kuṇḍalinī, when rising from* mūlādhāra cakra, *vibrates the six wheels* (cakras) *residing in the central path* (suṣumnā) *by supreme motion and brings them into existence.*[2] *By that supreme motion, She produces exquisite sound, which is filled with joy. Then She reaches the abode of Lord Śiva, Who resides in the*

1. This lecture was originally written by Swamiji in Sanskrit.
2. We have six (*ṣaṭ*) cakras but for us they are dead. They are there, but we cannot experience them, they are dead.

> *thousand-spoked wheel* (sahasrārdhacakra) *in the skull and, pleasing Him, pervades the whole universe. May this Kaulikī Kuṇḍalinī bestow upon you all the flows and streams of the state of universal bliss* (jagadānanda).

Kaulikī Kuṇḍalinī is that state of *kuṇḍalinī* described in the Kula system. Contained in Kaulikī Kuṇḍalinī is the threefold *kuṇḍalinī: prāṇa-kuṇḍalinī, cit-kuṇḍalinī,* and *parā-kuṇḍalinī.* Now, I will describe the nature and form of *kuṇḍalinī.*

Kuṇḍalinī is often considered to be the Creative Energy (*visarga-śakti*) of Lord Śiva. This Creative Energy of Lord Śiva, called *kuṇḍalinī,* is filled with complete I-Consciousness (*aham vimarśa*) and according to the Tantras it is coiled three and one-half times and rests in *mūlādhāra cakra.*

What are these three and one-half coils? I-Consciousness which is attached to objectivity is the first coil. I-Consciousness which is attached to the cognitive cycle is the second coil. I-Consciousness attached to subjective consciousness is the third coil. Where *pramiti* is residing in that I-Consciousness, that is its one-half coil.

What is *pramiti*? To understand *pramiti* you must first understand what *pramātā* is. *Pramātā* is that state of the knower where the knower is attached to the known, to the object. In *pramātā* there are traces of objectivity before the knower. Where these traces of objectivity are also dissolved in the state of *pramātā,* that state of *pramātā* is called *pramiti.* This is the secret of the Tantras.

When Kuṇḍalinī Śakti, the embodiment of the supreme Energy of I-Consciousness takes the support of Her free will (*svātantrya*), the whole manifestation of the universe takes place. How does this occur? The freedom of Kuṇḍalinī Śakti has three phases. In the first phase, Her freedom is directed toward objectivity (*bahiraunmukhya*). It is not resting in objectivity, rather it is at the point when it is just about to go outside. Here the tendency is toward objectivity, toward outward creation. It is this phase of Her freedom that is the main cause of the manifestation of the universe. The whole manifestation of the uni-

Plate 19. Swami Lakshmanjoo with George van den Barselaar.

verse takes place by means of this main cause, *svātantrya,* directed towards objectivity.

When She accomplishes this kind of action by the free Will (*svātantrya*) of Her Creative Energy, She is resting in her own nature. It creates in Her own nature and it exists in Her own nature. In this state, as that supreme Energy of God Consciousness, which has complete free Will, She perceives the whole objective world as one with Her nature. In this state the objective world is not separate from Her nature. Here She takes the form of a sleeping serpent. This state of *kuṇḍalinī* is called *śakti-kuṇḍalinī*. *Śakti-kuṇḍalinī* and the state of *kuṇḍalinī* called *prāṇa-kuṇḍalinī* are one. In all Tantras, *śakti-kuṇḍalinī* is described in this way.

> *She gives the light of consciousness to everyone, but she does not produce anything.*
>
> Tantrāloka 3:139

Śakti-kuṇḍalinī is the producer of light (*prakāśa*) in everyone. Here the word "light" means knowledge consciousness. In the individual this light is produced in five classes. The light of sound (*śabda*), the light of touch (*sparśa*), the light of form (*rūpa*), the light of taste (*rasa*), and the light of smell (*gandha*). These are the five classes. And these five classes are not the only light. Light is also found in the five sensations: the sensation of seeing, the sensation of touch, the sensation of hearing, the sensation of smelling, and the sensation of taste.[3] She produces this light, and yet actually She has not come out from her nature. She is resting there in her own nature. Although it seems to everyone that she has stepped out of her nature she has not. And yet, She is not lost. Although you see all of this manifestation, this manifestation resides in Her own nature. In the center of Her own nature, She has not gone astray.

This essense of creativity is just the splendor of Her own nature of complete independence (*svātantrya*). And, although it is creative, nothing is created. She relishes the taste of Her own glorious nature. This relishing is designated as the Energy of Lord Śiva, which, in Her own nature, takes the form of the first sprout that gives rise to the manifestation of the universe of one hundred and eighteen worlds. And as it sprouts, so it can be withdrawn.

According to the statement of Śaiva scriptures, when a *yogī* takes the support of attentive awareness and meditates on the nature (*svarūpa*) of Śiva—which is one with the *yogī's* own nature—and when that *yogī* achieves the state of absorption (*samāveśa*), that absorption is such that it dissolves the whole universe in his own nature. When this *yogī* meditates in this way he achieves the Creative Energy (*visarga-śakti*) of Lord Śiva and perceives the state of the supreme movement (*spanda*) of Energy in his own nature. He then gains entry into the state of *śakti-kuṇḍalinī*.

The nature of *śakti-kuṇḍalinī* is described in the *Tantrasadbhāva* as follows:

---

3. Here the light (*prakāśa*) of sound, or of any sensation, refers to the knowledge or awareness of that sensation. On the other hand, light can also be understood as the sensing itself—as hearing, seeing, smelling, tasting, and touching.

That Energy, supreme and subtle, is above the boundary of caste. It resides in each and every human being protecting their real heart (hṛidbindu). *There, taking the form of a sleeping serpent,*[4] *She embraces that heart in her own nature. O Pārvati! There She rests in deep sleep. She does not understand anything except Her own nature. Although She takes the moon, fire, sun, all the stars, and all the fourteen worlds, and makes them rest in Her own body, that Goddess (devī) appears just as if She had lost consciousness because of some heavy intoxicant or poison.*

That *śakti-kuṇḍalinī* is described as follows in the *Tantrāloka*:

The seventeenth kalā *is filled with the embodiment of supreme nectar.*[5]

Tantrāloka 3:138a

---

4. This point of the heart, which is the real heart, does not only reside in the heart, it resides in the center of all the six wheels (*cakras*) right from the *mūlādhāra cakra* to the *sahasrārdha cakra*. The center of the *mūlādhāra cakra* is the heart, the center of the navel (*nābhi*) *cakra* is the heart, the center of the heart (*hṛit*) *cakra* is the heart, the center of the throat (*kaṇṭha*) *cakra* is the heart, the center of the eyebrow (*bhrū-madhya*) *cakra* is the heart, and the center of the one-thousand spoked (*sahasrārdha*) *cakra* is the heart.

5. In Śaiva philosophy the world of experience is likened to the moon which has fifteen phases. There is also a sixteenth phase and this sixteenth phase is known as the sixteenth *kalā*. It is called *amākalā*, that phase of the moon that is never reduced. It is that phase of the moon that is ever-present even during the dark phase of the moon. The seventeenth *kalā* is above even that. The seventeenth *kalā* refers to the flowing out of the universal nectar of God Consciousness. It is called the seventeenth because it has nothing to do with the objective world, the cognitive world, or the subjective world. It is above all of these.

The Creative Energy (*visarga-śakti*), *śakti-kuṇḍalinī*, is also known as the medium energy (*parāparā-śakti*[6]) of Lord Śiva. This energy is the seed (*bīja*) of all other energies because it is from here that they flow forth. The supreme state of *visarga-śakti* is supreme (*parā*) *kuṇḍalinī* and the last state of *visarga-śakti* is *prāṇa-kuṇḍalinī*.

Kāma-kalā

Now I want to clarify for you the important and often misunderstood event known as *kāma-kalā*. *Kāma-kalā* refers to the conjunction or togetherness of the two aspects of any sensation, whether it be tasting, enjoying, or touching. All these are *kāma-kalā*. The conjunction of two (*kāma*)[7] does not only refer to sex as some would believe. The conjunction of two does exist in the sexual act, but it also exists when the eye is united with form. It also exists when the ear is united with sound, the nose united with smell, the skin united with touch.

The aspirant of the Kula system[8] is meant to experience the state of *kāma-kalā*. The Kaula aspirant meditates on these conjunctions in their various manifestations. He meditates on them in the sexual act, and he meditates on them in form (*rūpa*), in taste (*rasa*), in sound (*śabda*), in touch (*sparśa*), and in smell (*gandha*). Everywhere in these unifications, in these conjunctions, he experiences the state of *kuṇḍalinī*. This is called *caryā-krama*, which is succession (*krama*) in the activity (*caryā*) of the senses.

---

6. The medium energy (*parāparā-śakti*) of Lord Śiva, which is *visarga-śakti*, becomes three energies. The first energy is supreme energy (*parā-śakti*), the second energy is medium energy (*parāparā-śakti*), and the third energy is inferior energy (*aparā-śakti*).

7. The word *kāma* ordinarily means "desire." Here, Swamiji is using the word *kāma* in a special technical sense, referring to the desire that leads to the conjunction of two things.

8. The Sanskrit word *kula* means "totality." The Kula system was originally introduced in Kashmir in the beginning of the fifth century C.E. by Śrīmacchandanātha. As time passed this teaching began to fade away. Then, in the beginning of the ninth century it was reintroduced in Kashmir by the great sage Sumatinātha. The disciple of Sumatinātha was Somanātha, and his disciple was Śambhunātha. The disciple of Śambhunātha was Abhinavagupta.

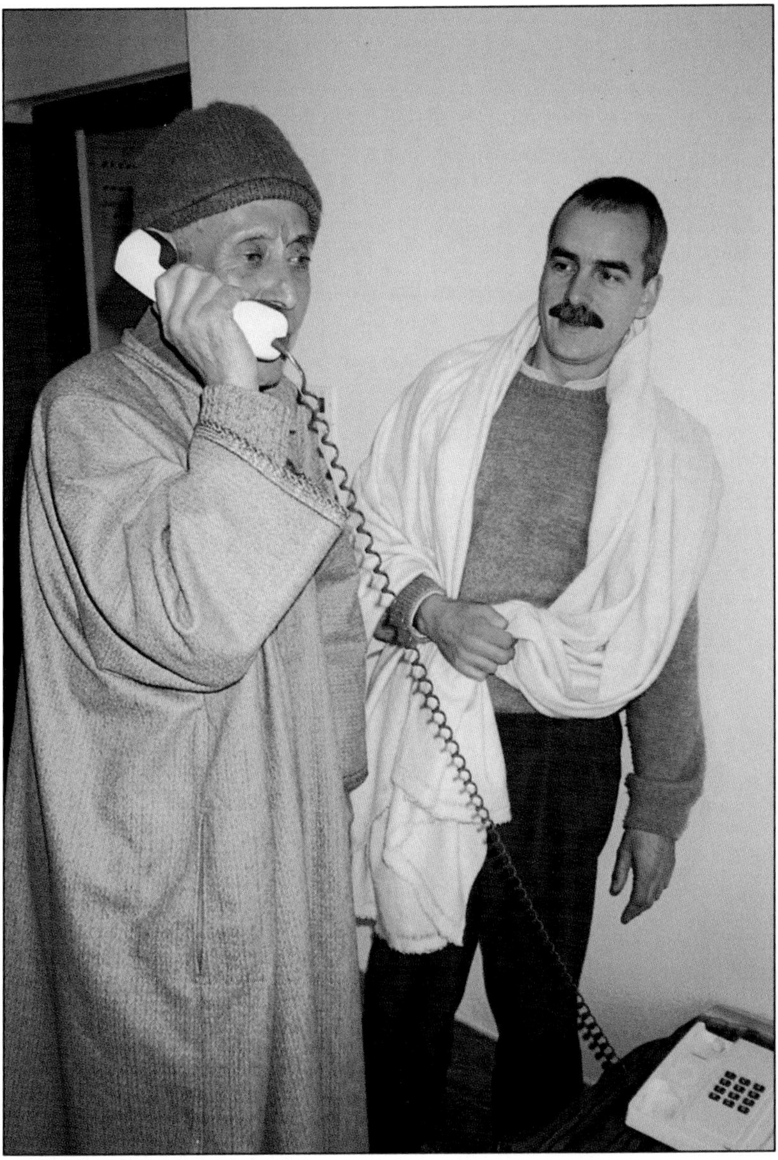

Plate 20. Swami Lakshmanjoo with Jonathan Abraham.

Śakti-kuṇḍalinī is experienced by this Kaula *yogī* when he enters the absorption (*samāveśa*) of *siddha-yoginī*.[9] The traditional understanding of *siddha-yoginī* is that it refers to the unification of two people such as occurs in the sexual act: *siddha*, the male element, and *yoginī*, the female element. This is the customary meaning of *siddha-yoginī*. But the absorption of *siddha-yoginī* can also takes place at the conjunction, the unification, of any two perceptions. It can take place in that unification where *siddha* refers to the eyes and *yoginī* the form, or *siddha* can be the ear and *yoginī* the sound. I am not referring to the physical eye or physical ear, but to the energy of seeing and the energy of hearing. Physical seeing or hearing is not the energy of seeing or hearing. For meditation in *caryā-krama* the sensation of the knowledge of this cognition (*jñānendriyas*) is utilized. This is known as the reality of *kāma-tattva*.

Our great teacher Abhinavagupta has also clarified this in his *Tantrāloka*:

> *In the* Kulaguhvara Tantra *we are told that the energy of Creation* (visarga) *is found in all conjunctions because it is the creative energy. By the contact of two, something else is created. It may be joy, it may be satisfaction, but something is created. This energy of Creation* (visarga) *is the letter* ḥ.[10] *This letter is a half letter and is only partly produced. It is not a complete* "ha." *This* ḥ *which is indistinctly produced is called the reality* (tattva) *of* kāma[11] (*willful desire*) *because* kāma *is only fulfilled when it is united. When it is united that is the true state of* kāma.
>
> Tantrāloka 3:146

---

9. The words *siddha-yoginī* literally mean male adept (*siddha*) and female aspirant (*yoginī*).

10. See chapter 3, page 68.

11. In Śaivism *kāma* means *icchā*, will. *Kāma-tattva*, the essence of will, is that will that is not generated. When *kāma* is not generated it is will. When *kāma* is generated then that *kāma* is desire. When it is generated, it rises. When it is not generated, it is there. It is like the ocean. There are numberless waves on the ocean, and although these waves appear, there is nothing other than the ocean. So it is with Lord Śiva. Everything has been created yet nothing is created.

In the *Vātūlanātha Sūtra* we are also taught:

> *Supreme unification takes place through the contact of* siddhas *and* yoginīs. *This is the great festival of unification* (mahāmelāpa).

The truth is that all contacts are sexual. So this verse not only refers to physical sexual contact, it refers to all sensual contacts. In this way, hearing is a sexual contact. Seeing is a sexual contact. Smelling is a sexual contact. Touching is a sexual contact. Tasting is a sexual contact. So in this verse, the word *siddha* refers to I-Consciousness and the word *yoginī* refers to whatever objectivity united with it.

The word *mahāmelāpa* in this verse means "festival of supreme meeting." This describes that state of *śakti-kuṇḍalinī* where the supreme meeting of Śiva and Śakti takes place. If that fortunate Kaula *yogī* achieves and experiences this state of *śakti-kuṇḍalinī* for only one second, then he has achieved the unification of Śiva and Śakti. This is that state where Śiva and Śakti cannot be distinguished from each other (*mahāsāmarasya*), where the individuality of Śiva and Śakti is lost. Śiva is everywhere and Śakti is everywhere. It is just like mixing together two containers of milk in one pot. These two containers of milk, once united, cannot be separated. This is the state of that supreme union where Śiva and Śakti become one with each other, where they cannot be experienced separately. In that state of the great festival of union (*mahāmelāpa*), which takes place by the contact (*saṁghaṭṭa*) of *siddhas* and *yoginīs,* the Kaula *yogī* perceives the state of *śakti-kuṇḍalinī* and can hereafter do whatever he likes. Henceforth there is no sin for him in any action.

You must clearly understand that only this *yogī,* and no one else, is fit to practice *caryā-krama.*[12] This means that only those *yogīs* who are established in the awareness (*vimarśa*) of their nature as Śiva, who have hearts as broad as the ocean, and who are seated in that state that is above all, have the right to practice *caryā-krama.* Others who try to practice it without these

---

12. The practice of *caryā-krama* is the practice of entering into the Supreme through sensual contact. This is not merely sensual contact but sensual contact filled with knowledge.

qualifications will only fail and cause themselves difficulties.

In this connection, Kṣemarāja wrote the following verse:

> *If those* yogīs *who falsely imagine that they are Kaula* yogīs *attempt* caryā-krama, *they will not be able to hold it. They are not fit for this communication, the rising of* śakti-kuṇḍalinī. *To experience this state of* caryā-krama *a* yogī *must possess a heart complete in fullness. He must be broad-minded like an ocean, for it is an ocean where all moving streams become unmoving and soundlessly rest.*
>
> Spanda Nirṇaya

So when this *yogī,* on the occasion of the co-union of *siddhas* and *yoginīs,* which occurs during the practice of *caryākrama,* touches *kāma-kalā*[13] and gains entry into *viṣa-tattva,*[14] he will experience the state of *prāṇa-kuṇḍalinī.* This *viṣa-tattva* is the state of the great meeting of *siddhas* and *yoginīs* called *mahāmelāpa.* In the divine scriptures it is also called *kāma-tattva* because, in both cases, it is the grasping of the moment of union.

---

13. *Kāmakalā* is the technique of grasping the moment of the union (*saṁghaṭṭa*) of the senses and their objects.

14. As Lord Śiva explains to Śakti in the *Kulaguhvara Tantra,* His state of Śiva and Śakti is just like two halves of a crow's beak (*kākacañcupuṭa*) because they are just one over the other. They should remain as one and not be separated. I-ness and this-ness should remain as one. As one, this-ness is not found separate from I-ness and I-ness is not found separate from this-ness. Also in the sexual act, a woman is not found separate from a man or a man found separate from a woman. It is not just the actual sexual act that is sexual. All sensory experience is sexual. This is *viṣa-tattva. Viṣa-tattva* is the state of being where you are either given to expansion or to the state of contraction. In Śaivism the word *viṣa* is explained in two ways. The word *viṣa* means, literally, "poison." When you are in the sexual act (*viṣa-tattva*) and you are elevated and situated in the expansion of your nature then at the very moment of union you will gain entry in *kuṇḍalinī.* If, however, you are given to the sexual act, then this sexual act will cause you to fall. This is also *viṣa-tattva* but in this case you are carried away from your nature. So in *viṣa-tattva,* when, in that act, you do not get entry into your nature, that act is poison for you. For those who are elevated this same poison is actually ecstasy (*amṛita*).

Plate 21. Swami Lakshmanjoo with Denise Hughes.

Prāṇa-kuṇḍalinī

Now I will explain the nature of *prāṇa-kuṇḍalinī*.

This Creative Energy (*cit-visarga-śakti*) of Lord Śiva is filled with the taste of Her consciousness.

> *The nature of* visarga-śakti *is to create one's own self from one's own Self in one's own Self.*
>
> Tantrāloka 3: 141

To create the self from the Self in the Self is the reality of Creative Energy (*visarga-śakti*).

Abhinavagupta tells us that when *kuṇḍalinī* experiences the state of the Creative Energy of consciousness in Her own nature then, in the very beginning of creation, breath (*prāṇa*) comes forth as the first creation. This is not the physical breath. It is the vibrating breath of life (*prāṇana*). This first manifestation of *visarga-śakti* is the seed of *prāṇa*. This is the stage of the vibrating breath, the breath of life called *prāṇana*.

When the consciousness of God Consciousness descends, when this consciousness flows out in the creative cycle, She takes the form of vibrating breath. What is this breath? As an example, take the creation of life within a woman. When a woman conceives a child, that child is first produced with this vibrating breath. At that time there is no actual breathing, there is only life. That is vibrating breath. When this Creative Energy (*visarga-śakti*) has taken the form of vibrating breath (*prāṇana*), the scriptures tell us that this breath is in the form of *prāṇa-kuṇḍalinī*.

In the next movement of this vibration the five states of breath—*prāṇa, apāna, samāna, udāna* and *vyāna*[15]—begin to form. At this stage, however, these five breaths are not yet manifested. Because of this, you will only find at this stage the state

---

15. *Prāṇa* is breathing in and out, *apāna* exists when you go to bathroom and push out your excrement or urine. *Samāna* is that breath which keeps your nerves in tune and all vital channels in balance. *Udāna* is the breath used to digest food in your body. *Vyāna* is the breath that stimulates all this and directs it with vibrating force.

of *prāṇa-kuṇḍalinī.* In this state of *prāṇa-kuṇḍalinī* only the blissful state of one's nature appears.

This Energy of Consciousness (*cit-śakti*), which is in the form of *prāṇa-kuṇḍalinī*, appears in the first state of the creative pulse (*visarga*). The *yogī* understands this. He has experienced it.

According to the *Spanda Kārikās,* verses 24 and 25, Vasugupta tells us that the center of the two breaths is the way. Through this way you will gain entry in rising. In ordinary life (*vyāvahāra*) this way is closed and blocked. It does not seem passable. Still it will open when *prāṇa-kuṇḍalinī* occurs. When the supreme energy of consciousness is concentrated in *ūrdhva-mārga,* where the breathe neither goes out or in, you are carried to, and rest in, the center. This center is *ūrdhva-mārga*. When you concentrate on that *ūrdhva-mārga* with continual awareness, the incoming breath (known as *candra*, the moon) and the outgoing breath (known as *sūrya,* the sun) spontaneously enter in the pathway of the central channel (*suṣumnā*) and rush down to *mūlādhāra cakra*. Then, as *kuṇḍalinī*, it rises from the *mūlādhāra* to the *sahasrārdha cakra*. Passing through the subtle opening of *brahmarandhra*[16] it leaves the entanglements of this body and enters that infinite expanse of God Consciousness. Here breathing in and breathing out no longer exist. In this state you must give wholehearted, one-pointed attention to that vibrating center. If you divert your consciousness from that point for one moment, you will suddenly come out of that state and fall in the void state called *pralayākala*. At that point you will not yet be in the diverse cycle of the world filled with thoughts, you will be in voidness (*śūnya*). After falling into the void state you will open your eyes and again be as an ordinary person.

Now I will explain *prāṇa-kuṇḍalinī* to you according to my own experience. To achieve this highest state you cannot practice half-heartedly for a half an hour in the morning and a half an hour in the evening and a hour at midnight. That won't help you. You have to do it with continuity. Otherwise there is no hope in this life, there is only hope in the next life.

---

16. At the point of *brahmarandhra* there is a subtle opening. Through this subtle opening the *kuṇḍalinī* departs from the entanglements of this body.

The reality is that the whole universe is filled with Consciousness, and yet that Consciousness is lost to everyone. That is the cause of our being thrown in the cycle of *māyā,* filled with manifold tortures, and forced to experience the pain of disease and repeated births and deaths. That *yogī* who is always attentive (*prabuddha*) in this state will not lose his consciousness even if he were put under an anesthetic. The maintenance of attentiveness is a truly great thing. Vasugupta explains all this in his *Spanda Kārikās*. When this Śaiva *yogī* does not allow awareness to be absent for even one moment, remaining always one-pointed, established in the state of Śiva, directing his mind towards the state of absorption (*samāveśa-daśā*), then by the power of his one-pointedness, both breaths—the breathing in and breathing out—spontaneously enter in the central channel (*suṣumnā*).

After entering the central channel, the breath energy (*prāṇa śakti*) of this *yogī* attains the seat of the *mūlādhāra cakra*. And then, as *prāṇa-kuṇḍalinī,* it begins to rise in the central channel from *mūlādhāra cakra* towards the thousand-spoked *cakra* (*sahasrārdha*), the energy of breath (*prāṇa-śakti*) blooms on all sides and this *yogī* experiences the state of *prāṇa-kuṇḍalinī.*

Yogīs experience this state of *prāṇa-kuṇḍalinī* in two ways. For some *yogīs,* when the breath enters in the central channel the incoming breath (*apāna*) and the outgoing breath (*prāṇa*) initially descend (*adhomukha*). Here both ingoing and outgoing breath are naturally collected together. This is a spontaneous state where the breath is collected in one point positioned to descend. It is the state known as *lambikā*.[17] The state of *lambikā* cannot be established by any physical means because it is very subtle. There are four passages in *lambikā*. These two breaths, when they take the position of descending, arrive at the *lambikā* that is the passage from the right side. From left side there is another *lambikā*. The *lambikā* that exists on the left side is presently active in us while the *lambikā* that exists on the right side is blocked. At the moment when the incoming and the out-

17. There is a center called *tālu* in Sanskrit which is located in the roof of the mouth at the soft palate. In Śaivism this center is known as *lambikā-sthāna*, the place of *lambikā*.

going breath collect and take the position of flowing down, the breath stops. There is no breathing in and out. The ordinary course of breathing ceases, and you feel a choking sensation. Then the *lambikā* on the right side opens and the breath enters through that opening and rushes down.

When the breath gains entry through the *lambikā,* it produces a sound which is like that internal sound produced when you close the ears by pressing your fingers on them. It is a continuous sound like the sound of the ocean. A sound like this is produced when the two breaths gain entry into the central channel through the *lambikā* and travel to the *mūlādhāra cakra* where they rest.

At that point the *mūlādhāra cakra* is penetrated. At the *mūlādhāra cakra* there is a wheel—the Sanskrit word *cakra* means "wheel." When the *mūlādhāra cakra* is penetrated, the *yogī* experiences the wheel (*cakra*) beginning to move with great force and sound. It moves in a clockwise direction. This is the state experienced by *yogīs* at the first moment this occurs.

Here the breath no longer exists. It has taken the form of *kuṇḍalinī*. Now *kuṇḍalinī* advances from the *mūlādhāra cakra* and rises to penetrate the *cakra* residing at the navel, known as the *nābhi cakra*. At this *cakra* there also exists a wheel, and after being penetrated, this *cakra* also begins to move rapidly and make sound. At that time, the *yogī* does not feel that the *nābhi cakra* alone is moving; he feels that the *nābhi cakra* and the *mūlādhāra cakra* are both moving, just like wheels in a factory. Both *cakras* are moving and both are producing a sound. The *yogī* hears this sound and this sound produces joy. All this I am relating from my own experience.

Now from the *nābhi cakra* this breath travels in the form of *kuṇḍalinī* up to the heart and penetrates the *cakra* residing there. This *cakra* is known as the heart (*hṛit*) *cakra*. After being penetrated, this *cakra* of the heart also begins to move rapidly and becomes filled with sound. The *yogī* feels this. Here also, the *yogī* not only experiences the movement of the heart *cakra*. He experiences the movement of *nābhi cakra* and *mūlādhāra cakra* as well. He experiences and feels the movements of all three *cakras*.

In this way successively, breath in the form of *kuṇḍalinī* continues to rise and penetrates the *cakra* of the throat (*kaṇṭha*) and the *cakra* of *bhrū-madhya* found between the two eyebrows. With this penetration, both of these *cakras* begin to move rapidly along with sound. This is what the *yogī* experiences.

In this way the *yogī,* in this state of manifestation of *prāṇa-kuṇḍalinī,* experiences the movement of all these *cakras,* right from *mūlādhāra cakra* up to *bhrū-madhya cakra,* simultaneously just like a great machine. From that very moment, the *yogī* experiences the appearance of the eight yogic powers, *aṇimā,* etc.[18]

Those *yogīs* who are unfortunate experience the state of *prāṇa-kuṇḍalinī* in a second way. Their experience of the rise of *prāṇa-kuṇḍalinī* is the same as that experienced by great *yogīs* up to and including the experience of *lambikā* and the traveling from *lambikā* to the *mūlādhāra cakra.* At that point it is expected that from *mūlādhāra cakra, prāṇa-kuṇḍalinī* will rise, piercing the *cakras* beginning with the *cakra* of the navel, then the *cakra* of the heart, and so forth until it reaches and pierces *bhrū-madhya cakra.* But for the unfortunate *yogī* this does not happen. For this *yogī,* when *prāṇa-kuṇḍalinī* reaches the *mūlādhāra cakra* the rise of *prāṇa-kuṇḍalinī* is reversed and he at once experiences the *cakra* of *bhrū-madhya* in movement, not the *cakra* of the navel. After that he experiences the *cakra* of the throat (*kaṇṭha*) in movement. Both are moving simultaneously. Then he experiences the *cakra* of the heart in movement, and after that he experiences the *cakra* of the navel in movement. Finally, he experiences the *mūlādhāra cakra* in movement. All of these

---

18. The eight yogic powers (*aṣṭa-siddhi*) are *aṇimā, mahimā, laghimā, garimā, īśitva, prāpti, prākāmya,* and *vaśitva.*

Aṇimā is the power to become invisible. *Mahimā* is the power to become very large, to be able to produce a body like that of Hanumān. *Laghimā* is the power to become as light as a feather, so light that you can fly in the sky. *Garimā* is the power to become very heavy. With the power of *garimā* no power on the earth can move you. *Īśitva* is that power where you have sovereignty over this world. With this power there is no interruption of your will. Whatever you wish will take place. *Prāpti* is the power to be in different places at the same time. *Prākāmya* is the power over your own system. If you need to be hungry you will be hungry. *Vaśitva* is that power where everyone wants to be near you, where everyone is attracted to you.

cakras move with sound. When *prāṇa-kuṇḍalinī* rises in this fashion it is an indication that this *yogī* is attached to worldly pleasures. For him traces of attachment remain. This is the second way *kuṇḍalinī* rises, but actually it is not rising. It is falling.

For this *yogī* there is no chance of possessing the eight great powers of *yoga*. On the contrary, this *yogī* has entered into a state of absorption which is said to be devilish (*piśācāveśa*). It is not a correct absorption, and it causes this *yogī* to become the victim of an unending series of obstacles during the rest of his life.

Why does this happen? When it is not the will of Lord Śiva for *prāṇa-kuṇḍalinī* to rise properly, it does not rise properly. Everything takes place only when Lord Śiva wishes. According to the *Ratnamālāśāstra:*

> *When this state is established below, and when from there it penetrates higher and higher, that is the state of liberation* (mokṣa). *That is the state where* yogīs *become fittingly qualified for the attainment of knowledge. But on the contrary, when these states are penetrated downward from above and in reverse, that is incorrect absorption* (piśācāveśa). *That is the indication that hereafter this* yogī's *life will be filled with obstacles.*

Penetrating Initiation

The *yogī's* experience of the rise of *prāṇa-kuṇḍalinī* and the resulting penetration of the *cakras*—beginning with *mūlādhāra cakra* and ending with *bhrū-madhya cakra* or *sahasrārdha cakra*—can take many different forms. These spontaneous variations in the rise of *prāṇa-kuṇḍalinī* are known as "penetrating initiations"[19] (*vedha-dīkṣā*). This is explained in the *Tantrāloka* by Abhinavagupta:

---

19. "Penetrating initiation" comes spontaneously from *kuṇḍalinī* and not from the master. It is said to be "penetrating" because during the rise of *kuṇḍalinī* the cakras are pierced or "penetrated" in various ways depending on the spontaneous desire of the *yogī*.

Plate 22. Swamiji with Viresh Hughes.

> *This initiation of penetration is described in different ways in the Tantras. Here the* yogī *has to experience the initiation of penetration by which he rises from one cakra to another and simultaneously experiences these cakras in movement. By this, the eight great powers of* yoga *are possessed by* yogīs.
>
> Tantrāloka 29:237–238

In the *Kulaguhvara Tantra* penetrating initiation (*vedha-dīkṣā*) is said to be six-fold.

Mantra-vedha is first, *nāda-vedha* is second, *bindu-vedha* is third, *śākta-vedha* is fourth, *bhujaṅga-vedha* is fifth, and sixth is the supreme (*para*) *vedha.*

These six-fold penetrating initiations revealed in the *Kulaguhvara Tantra* all take place in *prāṇa-kuṇḍalinī*. When *prāṇa-kuṇḍalinī* rises from *mūlādhāra cakra* to *bhrū-madhya cakra* or *sahasrārdha cakra,* the state of the *yogī* and the impressions acting on him determine his experience. These six-fold penetrating initiations each reflect a different experience in the rise of *prāṇa-kuṇḍalinī*. The varieties of penetrating initiations come to the aspirant depending on his desires and longings.

Mantra-vedha, the first piercing, is that piercing where the *yogī* hears the sound of a *mantra*. This kind of piercing takes place when the *yogī* intensely desires and longs for the recognition of Supreme I-Consciousness. In this case, when *prāṇa-kuṇḍalinī* rises, it takes the form of *mantra*, and the *yogī* hears a *mantra* such as *oṁ, Śiva, aham,* or *so'ham*. At the same time, he feels: "I am this *kuṇḍalinī*. I am one with this *kuṇḍalinī*." This is called *mantra*. His breath (*prāṇa*) becomes full of bliss, ecstasy, and joy. By the power of complete I-Consciousness, this blissful breath penetrates all the *cakras* from *mūlādhāra* to *bhrū-madhya* or *sahasrārdha*. This kind of penetration is called *mantra-vedha*.

Another variety of piercing is known as *nāda-vedha*. This type of piercing occurs when the *yogī* desires to uplift people. There is an intense desire: "I am doing this practice solely for the benefit of mankind." Here, when the blissful force of breath touches *mūlādhāra cakra*, this breath is transformed into *nāda*. Literally the word *nāda* means "sound." It is called *nāda* because the *yogī* experiences the sound of a drum beating. "Dum dum dum," the constant sound of a drum is heard by this *yogī* during the rise of *prāṇa-kuṇḍalinī*. This initiation comes to the *yogī* who wants to explain the Universal Reality to others.

Another kind of piercing is called *bindu-vedha*. This type of piercing takes place when the *yogī* is attached to, and longs for, comfort, ease, happiness, and joy. Here the blissful force of breath is transformed into a fountain of semen. The word *bindu* means semen (*vīrya*). The *yogī* experiences that it is a fountain of semen which is rising from *mūlādhāra cakra* to *brahmarandhra* and spreading throughout his body. In *bindu-vedha* when the *kuṇḍalinī* rises, he becomes filled with joy and happiness. Sexual joy is nothing in comparison to the joy experienced in *bindu-vedha*.

Another variation in the rise of *prāṇa-kuṇḍalinī* takes place when the *yogī* has the desire to become strong and to maintain this strength. Here the aspirant experiences this rise from *mūlādhāra cakra* to *brahmarandhra* in the form of an ant because that blissful force of breath is transformed into energy. He feels that power is being developed. This is the rise of energy in *kuṇḍalinī*. He feels that he is the embodiment of energy. The sound is creating power. It is stimulating—indeed it is the greatest stimulation. Because this particular kind of penetration in *prāṇa-kuṇḍalinī* is filled with power (*śakti*), it is called *śākta-vedha*.

Bhujaṅga-vedha is that particular variety of piercing where, when *prāṇa-kuṇḍalinī* is rising, the *yogī* feels that a serpent is rising and producing a serpent sound. This kind of penetration takes place when the *yogī* has the impression that the form and reality of *kuṇḍalinī* is serpent power. In this case the rise of the blissful force of breath in the form of *prāṇa-kuṇḍalinī* takes the form of a cobra (*bhujaṅga*). He truly experiences that a cobra is rising, with its tail remaining in and touching *mūlādhāra cakra* and stretching to penetrate all of the *cakras* up to and including *brahmarandhra*.

Finally there is piercing known as *para-vedha*. *Para-vedha* is the supreme *vedha*. This *vedha* is experienced by those *yogīs* who are always bent upon finding the Lord and nothing else. They are not interested in this universe; they only want to give themselves completely to the Lord.

Supreme *Kuṇḍalinī*

Now we will touch upon the experience of supreme (*parā*) *kuṇḍalinī*. This supreme Creative Energy, *parā-kuṇḍalinī*, is experienced as one with supreme consciousness (*parā citi*).

When the supreme Creative Energy is directed towards Her internal nature (*svarūpā*), where all movement ends, She there relishes Her true state—the fullness of I-Consciousness (*pūrṇāhantā*) completely filled with God Consciousness. Then that I-Consciousness is diluted in consciousness-of-this, and consciousness-of-this is diluted in I-Consciousness. Here this fullness of I-Consciousness absorbs "thisness" and produces the oneness of internal *samādhi* and external experience (*vyutthāna*). Her own nature as the supreme Creative Energy and the world become one. They are experienced as being completely united, one with the other. There is absolutely no difference between them. This is the state of *krama-mudrā*. This is the state of *parā-kuṇḍalinī*. This is the state of *jagad-ānanda*.

In the *Tantrāloka* the definition of *jagad-ānanda* is given in this way:

> *Abhinavagupta says, "My master Shambhunātha described* jagad-ānanda *as that state that is completely unencumbered, where bliss* (ānanda) *is found shining, where it is universally strengthened by the Supreme I-Consciousness of God, and where the six limbs of* yoga—bhāvanā, dhāraṇā, dhyāna, pratyāhāra, yoga, *and* samādhi—*are no longer used or required."*
>
> Tantrāloka 6:51-52

Now, according to my own experience, I want to tell you something more about this. When a Śaiva *yogī* has become worthy of the supreme grace (*tīvra-śaktipāta*) of Lord Śiva, and when his energy of breath (*prāṇa-śakti*) enters in the pathway of the central channel (*suṣumnā*), it does not touch the six *cakras* that are found there. Rather, it rises without the interruption of these six *cakras*, just like fountain rising up to the thousand-spoked (*sahasrārdha*) *cakra*, and there it is filled with the bliss of God Consciousness. At that very moment this *yogī* experiences the state of absorption of *krama-mudrā*.

In the *Krama Sūtra* it says that a *yogī* first enters *krama-mudrā* in the introverted state. Then, owing to the intensity of *krama-mudrā*, he emerges from the introverted state and enters into the outer, external cycle of consciousness.

First, from outside, he goes inside, and then from inside he goes outside. This movement of going in and coming out and then again going in and coming out takes place by the force of the absorption (*samāveśa*) of *krama-mudrā*, not by the effort of the *yogī*.

Where the *yogī* travels from outside to inside and then from inside to outside, just to come to the understanding that outside and inside are not different aspects but one, that is *krama-mudrā*.

There is one more thing for you to understand. The one who experiences this state of the absorption (*samāveśa*) of *krama-mudrā* experiences this whole universe melting into nothingness in the great sky of God Consciousness (*cid-gagana*). Although he opens his eyes and perceives that everything is melting into that state, yet—when he strives to come out of that state—it becomes very difficult for him. As it is very difficult for us to enter into that state, in the same way, it is very difficult for that *yogī* to come out of it.

But why does he want to come out? He wants to come out for the fun of it, but he cannot come out. The intensity of God Consciousness does not let him come out. Yet he struggles to come out. Then for a moment he rises up, and after that he again, filled with intoxication, rests inside. Then, again, he strives to come out. He continues trying to come out and he gets out briefly but then again he is united inside. This happens again and again and this called *krama-mudrā*.

It is just like the actions of a swing, swinging back and forth, back and forth. One moment he comes out and in the next moment he rests in his own nature. By this process of *krama-mudrā* expressing the state of *kuṇḍalinī* inside and outside, he experiences the state of absorption (*samāveśa*) of supreme (*parā*) *kuṇḍalinī*. By this absorption the *yogī* of the Kula system enters that state which is pure, spotless, and without blemish (*nirañjana*).[20]

Here, there is no fear of death, no fear of falling, no fear of descending again into the world of limitation and bondage. This is the state known as *nirañjana-tattva*, the pure and spotless ele-

---

20. *Nirañjana* is one of three states. The first is *kāma-tattva,* the second is *viṣa-tattva*, and the third is *nirañjana-tattva*. The establishment of *viṣa-tattva* is *nirañjana-tattva*. The Sanskrit word *nirañjana* means "where there is no impression (*añjana*)." It is that state, that reality, that is pure and without blemish.

ment. It is the pathway of the energy of action (*kriyā-śakti*). So, in the end, the final *yoga* is the *yoga* in action. It is said, "When you find God in action, that action is pure and spotless (*nirañjana*), it is supreme."

So according to the ordering of *kāma-kalā, kāma-tattva* resides in the energy of will (*icchā-śakti*), *viṣa-tattva* resides in the energy of knowledge (*jñāna-śakti*), and *nirañjana-tattva* resides in the energy of action (*kriyā-śakti*).

When these three states are united with each other, when *kāma-tattva* is united with *viṣa-tattva* and with *nirañjana-tattva*, that is the state of *Bhairava*.

So, in the same way, the divine scriptures of our Śaivism (*śaivāgamas*) explain that the energy of will, *icchā-śakti*, is *śakti-kuṇḍalinī*. The energy of knowledge, *jñāna śakti*, is *prāṇa-kuṇḍalinī*, and the energy of action, *kriyā-śakti*, is *parā-kuṇḍalinī*.

Oṁ Tat Sat

Plate 23. Swamiji with Viresh Hughes.

APPENDIX A

Sanskrit Text of the Bodhapañcadaśikā

oṁ anastamitabhārūpa-
stejasāṁ tamasāmapi /
ya eko'ntaryadantaśca
tejāṁsi ca tamāṁsi ca // 1 //

sa eva sarvabhūtānāṁ
svabhāvaḥ parameśvaraḥ /
bhāvajātaṁ hi tasaiva
śaktirīśvaratāmayī // 2//

śaktiśca śaktimadrūpā-
vyatirekaṁ na vāñcchati /
tādātmyanayornityaṁ
vahnidāhikayoriva // 3 //

sa eva bhairavo devo
jagadbharaṇalakṣaṇaḥ /
svātmādarśe samagraṁ hi
yacchaktyā pratibimbitam // 4 //

tasyaivaiṣā parā devī
svarūpāmarśanotsukā /
pūrṇatvaṁ sarvabhāveṣu
yasya nālpaṁ na cādhikam // 5 //

eṣa devo'nayā devyā
nityaṁ krīḍārasotsukuḥ /
vicitrānsṛiṣṭisaṁhārā-
nvidhatte yugapadvibhuḥ // 6 //

atidurghaṭakāritva-
masyānuttamameva yat /
etadeva svatantratva-
maiśvaryaṁ bodharūpatā // 7 //

paricchinnaprākāśatvaṁ
jaḍasya kila lakṣaṇam /
jaḍādivilakṣaṇo bodho
yato na parimīyate // 8 //

evamasya svatantrasya
nijaśaktyupabhedinaḥ /
svātmagāḥ sṛiṣṭisaṁhārāḥ
svarūpatvena saṁsthitāḥ // 9 //

teṣu vaicitryamatyantam-
ūrdhvādhastiryageva yat /
bhuvanāni tadaṁśāśca
sukhaduḥkhamatirbhavaḥ // 10 //

yadetasyāparijñānaṁ
tatsvātantryaṁ hi varṇitam /
sa eva khalu saṁsāro
jaḍānāṁ yo vibhīṣakaḥ // 11 //

tatprāsādarasādeva
gurvāgamata eva vā /

śāstrādvā parameśasya
yasmāt kaṣmādupāgatam // 12 //

yattattvasa parijñānaṁ
sa mokṣaḥ parameśatā /
tatpūrṇatvaṁ prabuddhānāṁ
jīvanmuktiśca sā smṛitā // 13 //

etau bandhavimokṣau ca
parameśasvarūpataḥ /
na bhidyete na bhedohi
tattvataḥ parameśvare // 14 //

itthamicchākalājñāna-
śaktiśūlāmbujāśritaḥ /
bhairavaḥ sarvabhāvānāṁ
svabhāvaḥ pariśīlyate // 15 //

sukumāramatīñśiṣyā-
nprabodhayitumañjasā /
eme'bhinavaguptena
ślokāḥ pañcadaśoditāḥ // 16 //

APPENDIX B

Sanskrit Text of the Parāprāveśikā

viśvātmikāṁ taduttīrṇāṁ
hṛidayaṁ parameśituḥ /
parādiśaktirūpeṇa
sphurantīṁ saṁvidaṁ numaḥ //

iha khalu parameśvaraḥ prakāśātmā, prakaśāśca vimarśa svabhāvaḥ, vimarśo nāma viśvākāreṇa viśvaprakāśena viśvasaṁharaṇena ca akṛitrimāham iti visphuraṇam / yadi nirvimarśaḥ syāt anīśvaro jaḍaśca prasajyet / eṣa eva ca vimarśaḥ-cit, caitanyaṁ svarasoditāparāvāk, svātantryaṁ, paramātmano mukhyamaiśvaryaṁ, kartṛitvaṁ, sphurattā, sāro, hṛidayaṁ, spandaḥ ityadiśabdairāgameṣūdghoṣyate, ata eva akṛitrimāhamiti-satattvaḥ svayaṁprakāśarūpaḥ parameśvaraḥ pārameśvaryā śaktyā śivādi dharaṇyantajagadātmanā sphurati prakāśate ca / etadevāsya jagataḥ kartṛitvamajaḍatvaṁ ca, jagataḥ kāryatvamapi etadadhīnamaprakāśatvameva, evaṁbhūtaṁ jagat prakāśarūpāt karturmaheśvarādabhinnameva, bhinnavedyatve'prakāśamānatvena prakāśanāyogāt na kiṁcitsyāt, anena ca jagatā asya bhagavataḥ prakāśātmakaṁ rūpaṁ na kadācit tirodhīyate, etatprakāśanena pratiṣṭhāṁ labdhvā prakāśa-mānamidaṁ jagat ātmanaḥ prāṇabhūtaṁ kathaṁ niroddhuṁ śaknuyāt, kathaṁ ca tannirudhya svayamavatiṣṭhet, ataścāsya vastunaḥ sādhakamidaṁ bādhakamidaṁ pramāṇamityanu saṁdhānātmaka sādhakabadhaka pramātṛirūpatayā cāsya sadbhāvaḥ, tatsadbhāve kiṁ pramāṇam? – iti vastusadbhāvamanumanyatāṁ, tādṛiksvabhāve kiṁ pramāṇam? – iti praṣṭṭarūpatayā ca pūrvasiddhasya maheśvarasya svayaṁprakāśatvaṁ sarvasya svasaṁvedanasiddham / kiṁ ca pramāṇamapi yamāśritya pramāṇaṁ bhavati tasya pramāṇasya tadadhīnaśarīraprāṇanīlasukhādivedyaṁ cātiśasyya sadā bhāsamānasya vedakaika-rūpasya sarvapramitibhājaḥ siddhau abhinavārthaprakāśasya pramāṇavarākasya kaścopayogaḥ / evaṁ ca śabdarāśimaya-pūrṇāhantāparāmarśasāratvāt paramaśiva eva ṣaṭtriṁśat-tattvātmakaḥ prapañcaḥ / ṣaṭtriṁśattattvāni ca, — 1 śiva 2 śakti 3 sadāśiva 4 īśvara 5 śuddhavidyā 6 māyā 7 kala 8 vidya 9 rāga 10 kāla 11 niyati 12 puruṣa 13 prakriti 14 buddhi 15 ahaṁkāra 16 manaḥ 17 śrotra 18 tvak 19 cakṣuḥ 20 jihvā 21 ghrāṇa 22 vāk 23 pāṇi 24 pāda 25 pāyu 26 upastha 27 śabda 28 sparśa 29 rūpa 30 rasa 31 gandha 32 ākāśa 33 vāyu 34 vahni 35 salila 36 bhūmayaḥ, ityetāni / - athaiṣāṁ lakṣanāni / tatra śivatattvaṁ nāma icchā jñānakriyātmakakevala pūrṇānandasvabhāvarūpaḥ paramaśiva eva / asya jagat sraṣṭumicchāṁ parigṛihītavataḥ parameśvarasya prathamaspanda evecchāśaktitattvaṁ apratihatecchatvāt, sadevāṅku-rāyamāṇamidaṁ jagat svātmanāhantayācchādya sthitam rūpaṁ sadāśivatattvam, aṅkuritaṁ jagadahantayāvṛitya sthitamīśvaratattvam, ahantedantayouraikyapratipattiḥ śuddha-vidyā, svarūpeṣu bhāveṣu bhedaprathā māyā, yadā tu param-eśvaraḥ pārameśvaryā māyāśaktyā svarūpaṁ ghūhayitvā saṁkucitagrāhakatām aśnute tadā puruṣasaṁjñaḥ, ayameva māyāmohitaḥ karmabandhanaḥ saṁsārī, parameśvarāda-bhinno'pi asya mohaḥ parameśvarasya na bhavet-indrajālamiva aindrajālikasya svecchayā saṁpāditabhrānteḥ, vidyābhijñā-pitair-śvaryastu cidghano muktaḥ paramaśiva eva / asya sarvakar-tṛitvaṁ sarvajñātvaṁ pūrṇatvaṁ nityatvaṁ vyāpakatvaṁ ca, śaktyo'saṁkucitā api saṁkocagrahaṇena kalāvidyārāgakālaniyati -rūpatayā bhavanti / atra kalā-nāma asya purūṣasya kiṁcit kartṛitāhetuḥ rāgo viṣayeṣvabhiṣvaṅgaḥ, kālo hi bhāvānāṁ bhāsanābhāsanātmakānāṁ kramo'vacchedako bhūtādiḥ, niyatiḥ mamedaṁ kartavyaṁ nedaṁ kartavyaṁ iti niyamanahetuḥ, etat pañcakam asya svarūpāvarakatvāt kañcukamiti ucyate, mahadādipṛithivyāntānāṁ tattvānaṁ mūlakāraṇaṁ prakṛitiḥ, eṣā ca sattvarajastamasāṁ sāmyavasthā avibhaktarūpā, niścayakāriṇī vikalpapratibimbadhāriṇī buddhiḥ, ahaṁkāro nāma-mamedaṁ na mam-edamityabhimānasādhanam, manaḥ saṁkalpasādhanam, etat trayamantaḥkaraṇam / śabda-sparśa-rūparasa gandhātmakānāṁ viṣayāṇāṁ krameṇa grahaṇasādhanāni śrotra-tvak-cakṣur-jihvā ghrāṇāni pañca jñānendriyāṇi / vacanādāna-viharaṇa visargānandātmakriyā sādhanāni paripāṭyā vāk-pāni-pāda pāyūpasthāni pañca karmendriyāṇi / śabda-sparśa-rūpa-rasa-gandhāḥ sāmānyakārāḥ pañca tanmātrāṇi / ākāśamava-kāśapradam, vāyuḥ saṁjīvanam, agnirdāhakaḥ pācakaśca, salilamāpyāyakaṁ dravarūpaṁ ca, bhūmirdhārikā,

yathā nyagrodhabījasthaḥ śaktirūpo mahādrumaḥ /
tathā hṛidayabījasthaṁ viśmetaccarācaram //

ityāmnāyanītyā parābhaṭṭārikārūpe hṛidayabīje'ntarbhūtam etajjagat / katham? yathā ghaṭaśarāvādīnāṁ mṛidvikārāṇaṁ paramārthikaṁ rūpaṁ mṛideva, yathā vā jalādidravajātīnāṁ vicāryamāṇaṁ vyavasthitaṁ rūpaṁ jalādisāmānyameva bhavati, tathā pṛithivyādimāyāntānāṁ tattvānāṁ satattvaṁ mīmā-ṁsyamānam sadityeva bhavet, asyāpi padasya nirūpyamāṇaṁ dhātvarthavyañjakaṁ pratyayāṁśaṁ visṛijya prakṛitimātrarūpaḥ sakāra evāvaśiṣyate tadantargatamekatriṁ, tataḥ paraṁ śudhavidyeśvara-sadā-śivatattvāni jñānakriyāsārāṇi śaktiviśeṣatvāt aukāre'bhyupagamarūpe' nuttaraśaktimaye'ntarbhūtāni / ataḥ paramūrdhvādhaḥ sṛiṣṭirūpo visarjanīyaḥ, naraśaktiśivātmakam trikam evaṁ bhūtasya hṛidayabījasya mahāmantātmako viśvamayo viśvottīrṇaḥ paramaśiva eva udayaviśrāntisthānatvātnnijasvabhāvaḥ / īdṛiśam hṛidayabījam tattvato yo veda samāviśati ca sa paramārthato dīkṣitaḥ prāṇān dhārayan laukikavadvartamāno jīvanmuka eva bhavati, dehapāte paramaśivabhaṭṭāraka eva bhavati //

APPENDIX C

Sanskit Text of the Kuṇḍalinī Vijñāna Rahasyam

svādhārādullasantī dyutividitamahādivyatejaḥsvarūpā
ṣaṭcakraṁ sphorayantī gatikṛitimadhuradhvānamāvedayantī /
prāpyeśaṁ toṣayantī daśaśatakamale vyāpya viśvaṁ sthitā yā
viśvānandapravāhān vitaratu bhavatāṁ kaulikī kuṇḍalī sā //

bhoḥ bhoḥ śaivāgamaniṣṇātāḥ śrotāraḥ!
adya mayā kuṇḍalinī vijñānaviṣayamadhikṛitya yathābuddhi yathāgurvāmnāyaṁca kiñcit prastūyate / sāvadhānatatayā tat śṛiṇvantu bhavantaḥ /
sāmānyarūpatayā pūrṇāhantārūpā śaivī visargaśaktiḥ kuṇḍalinīti kathyate, yā sārdhatrivalayākārā āmnāyeṣu pratipādyate / tatra prameyapradhānaṁ ahantārūpaṁ kuṇḍalinyāḥ prathamo valayaḥ, pramāṇapradhānaṁ ahantārūpatvaṁ dvitīyo valayaḥ, pramātṛipradhānaṁ ahaṁ svarūpatvaṁ tasyā tṛitīyo valayaḥ, tathāvaśiṣṭārdhavalayaḥ pramā-pradhānāhamātmaka ityasyā āgamikī rahasyaprakriyā / ityevaṁrūpā paravimarśātmāsau parā saṁvideva yadā bahiraunmukhya lakṣaṇāt svātantryāttattadrūpatayā'vavibhāsayiṣā svātmanyeva prollasati, tadā sā parā śaktirghaṭapaṭādibhāvaṁ svātmābhinnarūpatayā vimṛiśantī

suptāhisadṛiśī śaktikuṇḍa-linīti sarvāmnāyeṣu nigadyate /

yeyam-

prakāśya sarvavastūnāṁ visargarahitā tu sā /
Tantrāloka 3:139

iti śrī tatrālokoktanītyā visargarūpāpi visargarūpatā-manaśnuvānā svātmanyeva camatkṛitimayī śivasyādyonmeṣātmikā śaktirbhavati /

kiñca-

śaivaśāsanadṛiṣṭyā yadā yogī svātmābhinnaśivasvarūpa-parāmarśānusandhānavaśād-viśvātmasātkārarūpāyāṁ samśveśabhūmau tiṣṭhati tadāsya visargaśaktau samāveśo jāyate, yena sa paramaṁ śaktispandaṁ svātmani camatkurvan śaktikuṇḍalinī-daśāmāviśati /

śaktikuṇḍalinyāḥ svarūpaṁ tantrasadbhāve yathā –
yā sā śaktiḥ parā sūkṣmā nirācāreti kīrtitā /
hṛidbinduṁ veṣṭayitvāntaḥ suṣuptabhujagākṛitiḥ //
tatra suptā mahābhāge na kiñcinmanyate ume /
candrāgniravanakṣatrairbhuvanāni caturdaśa /
kṣiptodare tu yā devī viṣamūḍheva sā gatā //

śaiva śakti kuṇḍalinī bhagavatī śrītantrāloke

kalā saptadaśī tasmādamṛitākārarūpiṇī /

ityārabhya-

prakāśya sarvavastūnāṁ visargarahitā tu sā /
śaktikuṇḍalikā .... //

ityantaṁ nirupitāsti, parāparāśaktyaparaparyāyā visargaśakter-iyaṁ bījātmikā madhyamā daśā bhavati / asyā visargaśakter-ādyantadaśayorvarṇanaṁ prāṇakuṇḍalinī parākuṇḍalinī-nirūpaṇāvasare bhaviṣyati / kāmakalāparāmarśānusāreṇa kaulayogyapi caryākrame tāṁ śaktikuṇḍalinīṁ siddhayoginīsaṁghaṭṭ-ātmakasamāveśāvasare kāmatattvarūpatayā sākṣātkaroti /

yadāhurācāryābhinavaguptapādāḥ
ata eva visargo'yamavyaktahakalātmakaḥ /
kāmatattvamiti śrīmatkulagyhvara ucyate //
kāmasya pūrṇatā tattvaṁ saṅghaṭṭe pravibhāvyate //
Tantrāloka 3:146

śrīvātūlanāthācāryeṇāpi-
siddhayoginīsaṅghaṭṭānmahāmelāpodayaḥ

ityasmin sūtre mahāmelāpaśabdena seyaṁ śaktikuṇḍalinī nirūpitā / yasyāṁ kṣaṇamātramapi sthitiṁ prāpya kaulayogī vedyavedakātmaśivaśaktyatmadvayavigalanena tāṁ śivaśaktyātmamahāsā-marasyarūpāṁ sthitimanubhavati – ityasyāṁ siddhayoginī-saṅghaṭṭātmamahāmelāpadaśāyāṁ śaktikuṇḍalinīdaśāmanu-bhavan yaḥ kaulayogī caryākramamācarati, sa eva caryā krame adhikṛito asti, nānya ityavadhātavam / tasmāt paripūr-ṇasvātmāvamarśaniṣṭhānāṁ pūrṇāśayānāmevāsminnirutta-rasamāveśāspade caryākrame'dhikāro netareṣām /
yadāhuḥ śrīkṣrmarājapādāḥ-
te nātrādhikṛitāḥ paraiḥ punaridaṁ
pūrṇāśayaiścarvyatām /
Spanda Nirṇaya

atha prāṇa kuṇḍalinī svarūpaṁ nirṇīyate /

ciccamatkṛitirūpā visargaśaktiḥ
svātmanaḥ svātmani svātmakṣepo vaisargikā sthitiḥ /
Tantrāloka 3:141

ityācāryābhinavaguptapādoktanītyā svātmanyeva visargasyonmeṣa- daśāṁ parāmṛiśantī "prāk saṁvit prāṇe pariṇatā" iti nayena prāṇanarūpatāṁ cāvabhāsayantī prāṇakuṇḍalinī rūpatayāgameṣu nirūpyate / yadapyasyāṁ prāṇanakuṇḍalinī-rūpāyaṁ visargaśaktau prāṇanarūpatvādbahirbhāvāvabhāsan-ātmikā sthitirdṛiśyate; tathāpyatra parāṇādi-pañcavāhāsyānunmīlanāt svātmānanda-camatkṛitimayatvameva sarvataḥ pravartate / iyameva prāṇakuṇḍalinīrūpā citiśaktirvis-aragasyādikoṭyātmani svarūpe, sphuratītikaulayogibhiranu-bhūyate /

atra tu svānubhavasāramapi kiñcinmayā varṇyate

> tāmāśrityo'rdhvamārgeṇa candrasūryāvubhāvapi /
> sauṣumne'dhvanyastamito hitvā brahmāṇḍagocaram //
> tadā tasmin mahāvyomni pralīnaśaśibhāskare /
> sauṣuptapadavanmūḍhaḥ prabuddhaḥ syādanāvṛitaḥ //
> Spanda 24-25

iti śrīvasuguptapādapratipāditanayena yadā śaivayogī kṣaṇa-mapyavadhānaśaithilyamasahamānaḥ satatameva śivātma-bhāva-manusandadhānaḥ samāveśadaśāyāmunmukho bhavati / tadāsya svātmānusanddhibalādevobhau prāṇāpānau sauṣumne mārge layaṁ gacchataḥ / tadantaramasya prāṇaśaktirmūlā-dhārapadavīmāśrayate/ tasmānmūlādhārānmadhyo'rdhvad-mārgeṇa procchalantyāṁ vikasvarāyāṁ prāṇaśaktau yogī prāṇa-kuṇḍalinyavasthāmanubhavati /
atra yogināṁ dve gatī bhavataḥ / tatrādyyā yathā-keṣāñ-cidyadā prāṇāpānau madhyamārge layaṁ gacchatastadā prath-amaṁ tāvadadhomukhau santau lambikāsthānaṁ bhitvāṅ-gulipihitakarṇaghoṣavat dhvanantau mūlādhāra-cakraṁ vedhayataḥ–tadāsya yogino mūlādhāracakramukta-prakāreṇaiva saśabdaṁ pūrṇavegena parivartata iti yogī prāthmyenānubhavati / tato mūlādhāracakrāt utthitā mad-hyavāhinī prāṇaśaktir-dvitīyaṁ nābhisthānagataṁ cakraṁ vedhayati, yadvaśāt dvitīyamapi nābhicakraṁ vegena saśabdaṁ paribhramati / tadānīṁ yogī yaugapadyenānayoś-cakrayoḥ parivartanadaśām-anubhavati / tadanu asya yoginaḥ prāṇaśaktirnābhicakrāt samutthāya vegena hṛiccakraṁ ved-hayitvor'dhvaṁ gacchati / tadā sa yogī hṛiccakrasyāpi vegena parivartanadaśāmanubha-vati / tataḥ kaṇṭhasthānamāptā sā madhyavāhinī prāṇaśaktiḥ kaṇṭhasthānagataṁ cakramevaṁ bhrūmadhyasthānagataṁ cakrañca vegena vedhayati, yadvaśāt

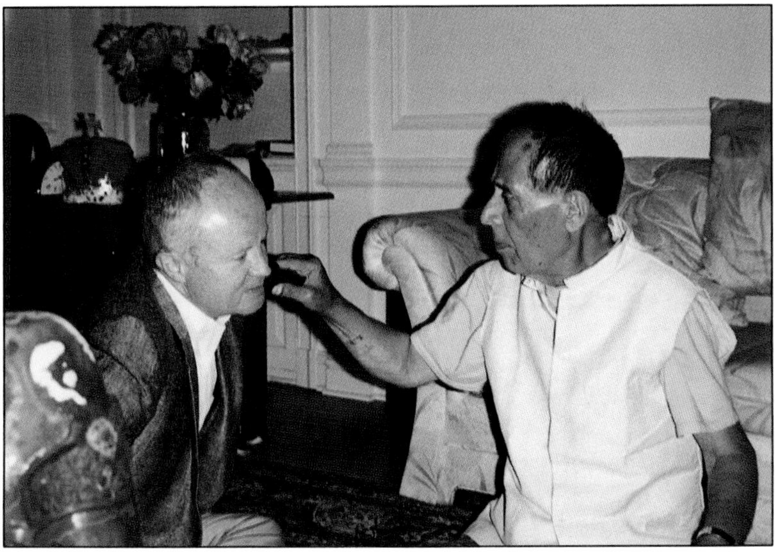

te ubhe cakre / api vegena parvartete-ityasya yogina evānubhavagocaratvameti / itthaṁ bindusthānagataṁ cakraṁ vedhayitvāyaṁ yogyasyāṁ prāṇa-kuṇḍalinīspandanadaśāyāṁ mūlādhāracakrashtānādārabhya bhrūmadhyasthānagata cakraparyantānāṁ samasthānāṁ cakrā-ṇām yaugapdyena savegaṁ parivartanarūpatvamanubhavati, yadantarmeva yogināmaṇimādyaṣṭasiddhayaḥ samāśrayante / amumevāśayaṁ vedhadīkṣāvicārāvasare ācāryābhinavaguptapādāḥ

śrītantrāloke upodvalayanti

> vedhadīkṣā ca bahudhā tatra tatra nirūpitā /
> sā cābhyāsavatā kāryā yeno'rdhvapraveśataḥ //
> śiṣyasya cakrasaṁbhedapratyayo jāyate dhruvaḥ /
> yenāṇimādikā siddhiḥ ... //
>
> Tantrāloka 29:237–238

atha aparā sṛitiryathā-
keṣāñcit ca mandayogināṁ madhyanāḍyāṁ yadā prāṇāpānā-

vastaṁ gacchatastadā teṣāṁ parameśvaraśaktipātasya mandatvādeva madhyavāhinī prāṇaśaktirviparyeṇaiva prathamaṁ bhrūmadhyasthānagataṁ cakraṁ vedhayati, yadvasādasya yoginastaccakraṁ prathamaṁ saśabdaṁ ghūrṇate tadanu kaṇṭhasthānagataṁ cakraṁ tato mūlādhārasthānaṁ yāvadakhilāni cakrāṇi saśabdaṁ parivartante yena tasya yoginaḥ saṁsāravāsanāyāstatrāvasthitatvena na kiñcidanubhava-gocaratvmeti / aṇimādi aṣṭasiddhīnāṁ kathā tu durāpāstaiva pratyut sa yogī nimnāṅkitena piśācāveśena samāviṣṭo bhūtvā vighnaparamparāmevānubhavati /

yaduktaṁ śrīratnamālāyam—

> adho'vasthā yadā ūrdhvaṁ saṁkrāmanti varānane /
> saiva mokṣapadāvasthā saiva jñānasya bhājanam //
> ūrdhvacakragatāvasthā yadādhaḥ saṁbhavanti ca /
> tadā paiśācaḥ āveśaḥ sa vai vighnasya kāraṇam //

atha kāmakalāṁ parīmṛiśan yogī siddhayoginīsaṅghaṭṭāvasarātmake caryākrama imāṁ prāṇakuṇḍalinīdaśāṁ viṣatattvapraveśasamaye'nubhavati / pūrvoktarūpāyāṁ mahāmelāpadaśāyāṁ yā daśā hyanubhūyate, saiva viṣatattvarūpāgameṣu varṇitāsti / śrīkulaguhvaratantre iyameva vedhadīkṣā mantranāda bindu śākta bhujaṅga paretirūpā ṣoḍhā varṇitā-

> mantravedhaṁ tu nādākhyaṁ binduvedhamataḥ param /
> śāktaṁ bjujaṅgavedhaṁ tu paraṁ ṣaṣṭhamudāhṛitam //

vedhadīkśāṣaṭakasya svarūpamadhastānnirdiśyate / mūlādhāracakrādutthitā pūrṇāhantātmakamantrasvarūpā prāṇakuṇḍalinī pūrṇāhantāvalāt samastāni cakrāṇi vedhayantī ādimā mantravedhadīkṣeti kathyate / madhyo'rdhvavāhakrameṇa ca procchalantī nādākārā sā dvitīyā nādavedhadīkṣeti bhaṇyate / vīryasvarūpā sā prāṇa kuṇḍalinī samastaṁ cakraṁ vedhayantī tṛitīyā binduvedhadīkṣeti nāmnā vyapdiśyate / śaktirūpātāmāpannā cakravedhanakriyāparā sā turyā śākta- vedhadīkṣā bhavati / sarpākāratāmādadhānā cakravedhanañca kurvāṇā vyuttiṣṭhantī bhujaṅgavedhadīkṣā pañcamī / parā-śak-

tirūpatāmāśrayantī samastacakravedhanaśīlā sā paravedhadīkṣā ṣaṣṭhīti /
atha parākuṇḍalinīsvarūpaṁ vimṛiśyate paracitirūpā visargaśaktiryadāntarbhāvaunmukhyarūpāntaḥ-koṭyātmani svarūpe svātmānaṁ camatkurvāṇā pūrṇāhantātmake pade idantāsamāveśaṁ tathedantātmake pade pūrṇāhantāyāḥ samāveśaṁ kurvatī samādhivyutthānasāmarasyadāyinīṁ kramamudrāyāṁ rūpāyāṁ jagadānanda-svarūpātmikāṁ parākuṇḍalinī-daśāyāṁ prakāśayati /

jagadānandasya lakṣaṇaṁ śrītantrāloka yathā-

yatra ko'pi vayavacchedo nāsti yadviśvataḥ sphurat /
yadanāhatasaṁvittiparamāmṛitabṛiṁhitam //
yatrāsti bhāvanādīnāṁ na mukhyā kāpi saṁgatiḥ /
tadeva jagadānandamasmabhyaṁ śambhurucitvān //

Tantrāloka 5:51–52

atrāpi svābhavānusāraṁ mayā kiñcillikhyate-tīvraśaktipātabhājanasya śivayoginaḥ prāṇā yadā sauṣumne mārge samāviśanti, tadā asya prāṇaśaktirmadhyo'rdhvavāhakrameṇa śaṭ-cakravedhana kramamaspṛiṣṭvaiva brahmarandhrasthānamā-sādya cidānanda- svarūpā bhavati / itthaṁ tasya yoginaḥ kramamudrāyāṁ samāveśo jāyate /

kramasūtreṣūktam—

kramamudrayā antaḥsvarūpayā bahirmukhaḥ samāviṣṭo bhavati sādhakaḥ, tatra ādau bāhyādantaḥ praveśaḥ, ābhyāntarādbāhyasvarūpe praveśaḥ āveśavaśājjāyate / iti sabāhyābhyantaro'yaṁ mudrā-kramaḥ /
kiñca- idṛiśīṁ samāveśadaśāmanubhava samāveśacamatkṛitibalādeva vyutthāne'pi samastaṁ bhāvajātaṁ cidgagane līyamānaṁ paśyan yogī yadā kiñcit kiñcit vyuttiṣṭhati, tadā tasya sar-vāṇīndriyāṇi prāṇāpānasahitāni kṣaṇaṁ prādurbhūya svātmanyeva līyante, itthaṁ sa hiṇḍolalīlāvadubhayataḥ prasar-antīmantarbahiḥ samāveśātmikāṁ daśāmanubhavanneva parākuṇḍalinīdhāma praviśati / yeno'rdhvakuṇḍalinīrūpāyāṁ kriyāśaktau samāveśo jāyate,

yadvaśāt kaulayogyapi siddhayogināsaṅghaṭṭavelāyāṁ nirañjanapadabhāg bhavati /

uktaṁ hi—

"kriyādevī nirañjanaṁ" iti

evaṁ kāmakalārahasyābhiprāyeṇa kāmatattvamicchāśaktau, viṣatattvaṁ jñānaśaktau, nirañjanatattvañca kriyāśaktāvantar- bahvanti / tathecchpśaktiḥ śaktikuṇḍalināti, jñānaśakti prāṇa-kuṇḍalinīti, kriyāśaktiḥ parākuṇḍalinīti ca tatra tatra śivāgameṣu vyapadiśyate /

Index